**To the Reader:**

The editors and publishers of The Long Riders' Guild Press faced significant technical and financial difficulties in bringing this and the other titles in the Equestrian Travel Classics collection to the light of day.

Though the authors represented in this international series envisioned their stories being shared for generations to come, all too often that was not the case. Sadly, many of the books now being published by The Long Riders' Guild Press were discovered gracing the bookshelves of rare book dealers, adorned with princely prices that placed them out of financial reach of the common reader. The remainder were found lying neglected on the scrap heap of history, their once-proud stories forgotten, their once-glorious covers stained by the toil of time and a host of indifferent previous owners.

However The Long Riders' Guild Press passionately believes that this book, and its literary sisters, remain of global interest and importance. We stand committed, therefore, to bringing our readers the best copy of these classics at the most affordable price. The copy which you now hold may have small blemishes originating from the master text.

We apologize in advance for any defects of this nature.

# The Glorious Adventure

## by
## Richard Halliburton

The Long Riders' Guild Press

www.thelongridersguild.com

ISBN No: 1-59048-084-8

The Author.

*To*

The Real Heroes of This Story

NELL AND WESLEY HALLIBURTON

My long enduring, ever courageous, infinitely patient
parents

As one that for a weary space has lain
    Lulled by the song of Circe and her wine
    In gardens near the pale of Proserpine,
Where that Aeaean isle forgets the main,
And only the low lutes of love complain,
    And only shadows of wan lovers pine,
    As such an one were glad to know the brine
Salt on his lips, and the large air again,
So gladly, from the songs of modern speech
    Men turn, and see the stars, and feel the free
        Shrill wind beyond the close of heavy flowers,
        And through the music of the languid hours
They hear like Ocean on a western beach
    The surge and thunder of the Odyssey.

**A. L.**

From *The Odyssey of Homer,* translated by S. H. Butcher and A. Lang; reprinted by permission of the publishers, The Macmillan Company.

# CONTENTS

# THE GLORIOUS ADVENTURE

# THE GLORIOUS ADVENTURE

## CHAPTER I

### THE GLORIOUS ADVENTURE

"Come, my friends,
'Tis not too late to seek a newer world.
Push off, and sitting well in order smite
The sounding furrows; for my purpose holds
To sail beyond the sunset . . . till I die . . .
To strive, to seek, to find, and not to yield."

"To STRIVE—to seek—to find—and not to yield"
caught my fancy as I sat before the fire with a volume
of Tennyson's poems opened to "Ulysses." What a
fine refreshing purpose,—"sail beyond the sunset till
I die." This clear call to leave behind the outworn,
too familiar life and seek a newer world found a
responsive chord in my own restlessness. I thought
to myself: Of all the great figures in history, did
not this royal vagabond who spent his days in
finding the extraordinary, in meeting new experience,
in knowing every thrill and beauty and danger the
world could offer—did he not have the fullest, the
richest, the most enviable life of any man who ever

lived? When the fates had spun his thread of destiny
to a close, how unregretfully he must have faced the
end! How proudly he could have said:

> *"I die content.* All times I have enjoy'd
> Greatly, have suffer'd greatly, both with those
> That loved me, and alone; on shore, and when
> Thro' scudding drifts the rainy Hyades
> Vext the dim sea: I am become a name;
> For always roaming with a hungry heart
> Much have I seen and known; cities of men
> And manners, climates, councils, governments,
> Myself not least, but honour'd of them all."

And more. He had ruled his island kingdom of
Ithaca in his youth; for ten years he had battled on
the ringing plains of windy Troy; he had sailed the
oceans with his ships, tasted of the lotus fruit,
struggled with the cannibal Cyclops, dwelt with
Æolus, the king of the winds, heard the singing of
the Sirens. He had braved the monstrous Scylla to
escape the whirlpools of Charybdis; he had even
descended into hell, before the intervention of the
gods brought him back home to his faithful wife—
and Ithaca.

As I thought of all this stirring drama, my own
life, imprisoned by apartment walls, surrounded by
self-satisfied people, caught in the ruts of convention and responsibility, seemed drab. In my own way
I too had been a wanderer. I had tasted the drug of

romantic travel, and I could not rest from it. I had
seen the sun rise over the Alps from the summit of
the Matterhorn; I had tramped the Pyrenees, and
basked in the warmth of Andalusia; I had watched
the moon sail across the sky as I sat enthroned upon
a fortress gun at the supreme summit of Gibraltar.
I had swum the starlit Nile, and from the apex of the
Great Pyramid waited for dawn to break. I had
loved a pale Kashmiri maiden beside the Shalimar.
From the high passes of the Himalayas I had seen
the roof of the world lifting up the heavens with
pillars of gleaming ice. The tropics I had known,
and the northern blizzards; and I had learned to love
the poetry and the majesty of the ocean from the
fo'castles of a dozen ships. I had "enjoy'd greatly,
suffer'd greatly, both with those that loved me, and
alone; on shore, and when . . . the rainy Hyades
vext the dim sea."

And now this slippered ease before the hearth—
how barren and profitless it seemed. How dull it was
"to pause, to make an end, to rust unburnished." I
rose from my deep chair and moved restlessly to the
window. The ships and the gulls were sailing down
the Hudson and out to sea; and I envied every sailor
that would wave farewell to the sky-line of New
York, and turn his salt-stung face to some strange
enchanted land beyond the far horizon. Suddenly
I became bored and impatient with everything I had

and was: bored with people, bored with knowledge
I realized I didn't want knowledge. I only wanted
my senses to be passionately alive, and my imagination fearlessly far-reaching. And instead, I felt I
was sinking into a slough of banality. Adventure!
Adventure! *That* was the escape; *that* was the
remedy. I knew there was no turning back once one
had broken from the nest of colorless security, and
spread one's own young wings, and visited the tall
strange tree-tops across the valley that had always
been beckoning.

I had once spread my wings,—and now that I had
returned to my nest again, I was dissatisfied. I had
security, and I did not want it; I had comfort, and I
did not enjoy it. I wanted only to sail beyond the
sunset. I wanted to follow Ulysses' example and
fill life once more to overflowing. Ulysses' example,—and then the idea flashed through my brain:
Ulysses' very *trail,* his *battle-fields,* his *dramatic
wanderings,*—why not follow these too!

My sudden enthusiasm for this glorious idea swept
away all practical obstacles. No matter if no one
knew exactly where the Sirens were,—I'd find them;
or if scholars disagreed about the Cyclops' cave—it
must be *some*where. I'd go to Ulysses' own island
of Ithaca and embark for the walls of Troy; I'd visit
Æolus and his cages of the winds; I'd brave the enchantments of the dreaded Circe; I'd swim from

Scylla to Charybdis and taste the lotus in the lotus land.

As I stood looking out upon the teeming Hudson, the whole smoldering idea caught fire: I must climb Mount Olympus to call upon the gods;—Delphi, to consult the oracle;—and Parnassus, to invoke Apollo;—Athens,—and the Hellespont,—and the classic isles of Greece. Homer would be my guide; the *Odyssey* my book. What matter if Greece were a barren waste—it would not be for me; or Troy a grass-grown mound of earth—*I* could see its lofty gates and its towers gleaming in the sun. Wherever Ulysses went, there I would go; across whatever sear he sailed, there would I follow. Why wait to embark? Below my window lies the port; the vessel puffs her sail; there gloom the dark broad seas. Come—Come—my friends,

> " 'Tis *not* too late to seek a newer world.
> Push off, and sitting well in order smite
> The sounding furrows; for my purpose holds
> To sail beyond the sunset . . . till I die . .
> To strive—to seek—to find—and not to yield

# THRONE OF GOD

# CHAPTER II

CRASH! The lightning in a rage split the writh‧ ing firmament from Thessaly to the Cyclades in one blazing, blinding glare. Streaks of fire burst into the inky darkness, inflaming the abyss about me and lashing at the clouds that hurtled past. The far-darting thunder, peal upon peal, roamed the Ægean Sea, plunged across the Vale of Tempe, and echoing back from the walls of Ossa, shook the granite rocks I sat on.

The wrath of Jupiter had burst upon me. Hidden by the seething darkness he charged across the sky, for I had violated the sanctuary of the immortals; in his wrath he flung the lightning at my head, for I had challenged his omnipotence; with his thunderbolts he sought to hurl me bodily back to earth, for I had dared to climb the utmost pinnacle of Mount Olympus and seat myself upon the very Throne of God.

Midnight was a strange hour to be on top Olympus. It was bad enough insolently dislodging

Jupiter by day from his own castle, but to cling tenaciously to it all night as well was nothing short of sacrilege. Small wonder he assaulted me so savagely. But how could I retreat! I was trapped ten thousand feet high, on top a towering rock chimney up the precipitous walls of which I had laboriously climbed that afternoon, clinging fearfully to the little crevices that allowed one to ascend only an inch at a time. It would have been suicidal, now that night had come, and the rain, and the clouds, and the lightning, to try to climb down. No, by all the gods, I would not, could not, move.

It was consoling, however, to know that if I were annihilated by outraged Jupiter, I would not suffer alone, for Roderic Crane, my American companion, and little Lazarus, a heroic half-grown shepherd boy who alone of all our retinue dared climb the final peak with us, stood defiantly by my side.

By desperate effort I was able to find amid all this darkness some small gleam of consolation. My position corresponded to that of a journalist whose house was wrecked over his head by an earthquake,—discomforting, yes, but magnificent copy. Roused by "the surge and thunder of the *Odyssey*," I had embarked resolutely upon Ulysses' trail in hope of finding some of the glorious adventure he had found so plentifully three thousand years ago. And here, at the very outset, was a reception to Greece, romantic

and tempestuous beyond my most extravagant hopes.
I felt that if this midnight battle with the gods was
a sample of the adventure in store for me, Ulysses'
shade would soon be looking on from Hades with
envious eyes.

Even before leaving far-away New York, Roderic
and I had chosen the pinnacle of Olympus for our
first great goal. The ascent of this immortal altar
was to be a pilgrimage in quest of atmosphere and
stage-setting, and of proper adjustment to the spirit
of our expedition. We had been born and bred in a
nominally Christian civilization where any heathen
belief in the efficacy of the ancient Greek divinities
was looked upon as a bit out of style. But if we were
going to revive the classic days of Homer and relive
the life of Ulysses, I felt it imperative (despite
Roderic's skepticism) to try to resurrect this fine old
fashion in religious faiths; I felt we should get
acquainted with Zeus* and Athena, with Hermes and
Neptune, who had been to blame for all the good and
all the harm that came to our hero. So we hastened
eastward to find and climb this deity-crowned
Olympus, "where the dwelling of the gods standeth
fast forever."

Our approach was from Salonica. On a hilltop

---

*No attempt has been made to be consistently Greek or consistently
Latin in the terminology of the classic gods. Sometimes I speak of
"Zeus," sometimes of "Jupiter." Generally I have tried to choose the
more familiar term.

behind this ancient city, we had looked southward and
first seen the most celebrated mountain in the world.
My pulse increased at the very sight of it—
Olympus—the far-off, unapproachable capital of
classic Greek mythology, and Greek art and culture
and life itself. To honor the gods of Olympus the
sublime temples of Greece rose in marble majesty;
in the image of Olympian gods the hands of Phidias
and Praxiteles gave posterity such sculpture that
each poor fragment is enthroned by modern art, and
guarded as a priceless possession. In the shadow of
Olympus, Homer sang the greatest poetry ever sung
before or since, and in the name of Mount Olympus
the most happy and sin-free religion the world has
ever known bloomed for centuries.

And yet I had always felt that Olympus, like the
other beautiful legends of ancient Greece, was only
a myth, a vague representation of divinity and immortality, which no longer really existed in this
iconoclastic age.

The view from Salonica disillusioned me, for now
a massive, purple, peak-ridged mountain loomed in
the distance, a ten-thousand-foot mountain touched
with snow and diademed in clouds; and that mountain,
as firm, as real, as tangible as the earth, was Olympus,
the golden throne of Zeus.

I was delighted to find it so beautiful. We saw it
first at twilight, when obscurity had invaded the

Mount Olympus loomed in the distance, a massive, purple, peak-ridged mountain, a ten-thousand-foot mountain touched with snow and diademed in clouds.

Painfully we climbed the shaggy walls of Mount Olympus' last grim battlement, clinging to this crack, feeling for the next crevice, not daring to look down at the clouds that were gathering below.

slopes, and the shadows were deepening in the gorges. But far above, its pinnacle still shone into the night, soaring toward the heavens, slowly—like a prayer.

For a long while Rod and I sat quietly, watching the picture fade. Then, without any warning, my companion asked me if I thought he would be alluring to Venus if we ever *did* get to the top.

"Yes, Rod," I replied a bit acidly, starting homeward as a gesture of remonstrance against his lack of reverence for poetic moments. "With your mustache and line of negro stories I'm sure you'll prove irresistible. Just the same, I want you to promise me you won't start any scandal with a goddess right at the beginning of our trip. Things are going to be complicated enough as it is."

Next day, scorning to waste another hour on crass material matters like equipment and provisions and directions, we hurried off to visit the gods, and at Larissa in Thessaly, on the opposite side of the mountain from Salonica, made ready for the grand assault.

The mayor, acting under official orders, much to our disgust attached a young army of gendarmerie to our train "to protect you from the bandits," whereas, next to the gods there was nothing in the vicinity we wanted to meet quite so much as these notorious Olympus bandits who have terrorized the district for generations. The idea of being romantically held up for ransom so captivated our fancy we had seriously considered advertising in the local paper for some gallant robber band that would oblige us.

And now the mayor had spoiled it all. We stormed against such a military burden. But all our protestations were in vain. So in ceremonial grandeur we moved Olympusward.

The second night found us sleeping on the ground at a shepherd's camp not far below the summit. Never shall I forget those Arcadian hours. We moved back two thousand years and lived again in classic pastoral Greece. The shepherds with their sunburned curls, in their coats of skin and felt, carrying their crooks, and playing their melancholy pipes amid their tinkling flocks might have stepped straight out of mythological literature. To make the setting truly a poem the full moon rose over the pine-clad summits that walled us in, and glowed upon our campfire, revealing the stilled herds upon the hillside and casting fantastic shadows among the rocks that might have been Pan and the Centaurs joined in their nightly dance.

It was on this night that Lazarus, the shepherd boy, annexed himself from out of nowhere to our retinue. We glanced up from our camp-fire to find him standing just inside the circle of light, with an expression of wonder and curiosity on his firelit face— foreigners—and such strange ones. He was leaning on his crook looking so shy, and yet so fearless; so wistful, and yet so self-sufficient. At close range he proved an extraordinary little satyr. He had never owned a hat other than his mat of sun-bleached hair; he had never had a home other than the hillside. He was as uncivilized as any of the half-wild goats he shepherded,—and as hardy. Whatever initial distrust the child had of us was changed to idolatrous worship when we expressed amazement and admiration on seeing him rake out several glowing embers from the fire and carry them in his bare calloused hands to another spot. Our compliments so touched his affection-starved heart that he was our very shadow until our climb was over and we had left him behind still in a state of high excitement over the greatest adventure that had ever befallen him.

Next morning in the sharp mountain air we moved in gay procession on up the canyon,—nine soldiers, fifteen shepherds, four mules, six dogs, two Americans—and Lazarus.

So far, the procession had proved much more interesting than the mountain. From Salonica, Olympus had appeared pinnacled and defiant. Now, at close range, all we had found was a rather barren hillside,—and here we were almost at the top—or so it seemed.

Never were appearances so deceiving. Our young shepherd-guide, realizing we had a shock in store, had rushed on ahead to the crest, calling back for us to hurry, hurry. When we gained the rim, there stood Lazarus, his piquant face a wreath of breathless excitement, his crook outstretched over a sudden canyon that dropped dizzily away, on the other side of which soared a fluted, stalagmite tower of naked sparkling rock. The great spire burst upon us so dramatically,—a smooth, swelling, mountain-side, and then, presto!—this amazing picture. We had been ascending only the shell of a vast and irregular amphitheater from out of the middle of which, a thousand feet below us, this arrogant tower sprang, to rise a thousand feet above.

No one needed to tell us that the spire was the throne of Jupiter. Several of the neighboring peaks, while almost as high, appeared to be easily scalable, but the summit of this one seemed as far beyond reach as heaven itself. The ancient Greeks felt they were safe in placing their gods on such an intimidating pinnacle-top, because it was past belief that any mortal man could climb its shaggy walls and shatter their theology. So right they were in believing the summit unconquerable that, though Olympus has been for three thousand years the most famous mountain in the world, the oldest in song and story, the heaven of a great and beautiful religion, it remained the last accessible mountain to be climbed.

Our crater crest was only a box-seat for all this

drama. That was not enough. We must have the stage itself. Our army captain insisted the peak was "impossible,"—only three times in three thousand years had it been surmounted by mortals.* We must have ropes, we must have guides, we must have permission from the army, we must have—we never heard what came next, because before he was well started on his "can't be's" and "must have's" Lazarus and Roderic and I were far down the jagged spur that connected our crest to the base of the tower, hellbent for the Homeric heaven.

We completed the descent into the intervening chasm and reached the great chimney. Scampering up it like one of the goats he tended, Lazarus beckoned us on. Painfully we followed him an inch at a time, clinging to this crack, feeling for the next crevice, not daring to look down at the clouds that were gathering below. Several times the shale gave way beneath us, and our hearts almost stopped as we looked into the gulch and saw how far an avalanche would take us.

Nothing made Lazarus stop. He moved relentlessly on, calling back encouragingly, returning to redirect our missteps, supplying such an abundance of moral support that he actually got us up the last grim battlement and led us with a shout over the top.

*The tower may have been climbed by people unknown to our guides. The surrounding peaks, offering no special difficulties, are frequently visited every summer.

Roderic looked eagerly about for Venus; I for Jupiter. Not one single god or goddess was to be found. This did not mean, however, that they had meekly abandoned the throne-room to the three infidels. We later learned that their disappearance was just a strategic move which would allow them to punish us all the more effectively.

Jupiter had seen us crawling like flies up to his inviolate sanctuary, and, realizing that we were determined to seize the summit, had flown away to marshal his armies of defense. In consequence when we did attain his empty throne a phalanx of black clouds with glowering faces was already sailing ominously past, entirely obscuring the long-anticipated panorama.

There was no time now for Roderic to lament Venus' lack of hospitality. The clouds were rapidly rising nearer and nearer from out of the chasm. Scarcely had we gained the summit when Lazarus began to implore us to escape from the chimney-top while the atmosphere was still clear enough to make descent possible. We could see the situation as plainly as Lazarus, but before we fled we were determined to leave behind a carved record of our conquest. On top a great flat boulder right at the point of the needle, the Swiss climber Boissonnas, who in 1913 was the first mortal to scale this highest tower of Olympus. had built a three-foot rock cairn as a monument to hi.

significant achievement. On the same boulder were the engraved names of the two other parties who followed. And here too, fog or no fog, our names, as the fourth party, must be emblazoned as a sort of visiting card for Jupiter when he returned.

Hurriedly we scraped away at the rock with our knives—closer crept the clouds. Lazarus became frantic at our indifference to the trap enclosing us. But we saw only the magnificent CRANE and HALLI-BURTON we were carving eternally into Jupiter's throne. The final E and N were completed. We pocketed our knives and harkened at last to Lazarus' wails of distress—too late. One sweep of the wind, and the fog, with startling suddenness, from all directions at once, had thrown its impenetrable blanket over us. We drew back from the brink, in alarm.

"Oh, it will soon pass by," I said encouragingly to Rod. "It's still two hours before darkness. Things will clear up in time."

"I hope so," he replied, shivering a bit from the damp clinging mist. "We really can't spend the night up here,—we haven't our nightshirts."

But things didn't clear up. The fog only grew thicker and wetter. Twilight was approaching, and in the secret mind of each of us apprehension was growing. We had left our coats behind with the soldiers, and already in the sharp wind that was driving the fog across our ten-thousand-foot perch, we were beginning to be uncomfortably cold. There was nothing we could do in the way of exercise to keep warm, for the needle's point was literally a point with abysses always just a few feet away that prevented our enjoying any resuscitating calisthenics demanding more floor space than deep breathing.

To keep up our spirits, Roderic resorted desperately to his banter. Under the circumstances it proved inefficacious, for Lazarus couldn't understand one word of English, and I was too occupied with anxiety to listen. Realizing his audience was reduced to one, he gave up, joined the gloom group, and waited for the most unwelcome night that ever enfolded Mount Olympus.

There was no hope of escape now till morning. We must protect ourselves as best we could in anticipation of a long and painful exposure. Some sort of shield against the biting wind would help a little, so the three of us, creeping cautiously through the fog on hands and knees, collected all the loose rocks we could find in the few square feet that measured our cage and piled them into a low wall abutting the boulder on top of which the Boissonnas cairn was built.

The cairn itself would have tempted us as a convenient quarry for building material, had the destruction of this historic monument not been the height of dishonor and the depth of sacrilege. Little in size and crude though it is, it marks one of

the symbolic episodes in the history of the world,—
the first ascent of the mountain of the immortals, and
the first overthrow of the king of all the gods from
this last refuge which, defending itself for three thousand years, had defied, by its precipitous walls and
surrounding chasms, the assaults of every unbeliever.

No, there were enough other rocks. And when
these were in place, we raised over them Lazarus'
shepherd's crook (which he had clung to all the way
up), decorated at the top by my red bandana handkerchief, our flag of conquest.

Night came all too soon,—black, grim, threatening. Roderic and I had Lazarus to worry about now.
We reasoned that his resistance to the exposure,
which we simply must endure till morning, was not
as strong as ours. We reasoned wrongly, for the
young shepherd very shortly made it clear that his
only apprehension was for *our* safety. And when I
recalled his method of transporting live coals, and
his mop of sunburned hair, and his wind-tanned face,
I came to the conclusion that if any one of us survived
the night it would probably be boy-Lazarus.

It was eight o'clock now. The sun would rise
about five. Nine hours of this! We may as well relax to the situation, keep our circulation going and
try to enjoy what we couldn't avoid. The summer
was well advanced, so that the temperature would
hardly drop to freezing. If the weather got no worse
it would be merely a matter of enduring a cold dis-

agreeable nine hours,—not of endangering life or limb.

The weather did get worse, much, much worse. Jupiter was only imprisoning us with the fog. And now that we were helplessly pinned to the needle-point, he prepared to charge furiously with every element at his command and sweep these usurpers over the brink.

At nine o'clock, with one frightful crash of lightning the outraged god sounded the charge, leaped into his chariot and, lashing his mighty horses, drove thundering upon us. His first hurled bolt missed its mark, ripped past us and struck the wall across the canyon, shattering a portion of it and sending the fragments dashing down the precipice. On rolled the Olympian cavalry of clouds to blanket the mountain anew in a fresh barrage of mist. The battalion of winds charged against our bastion, overhurling our flagstaff and slashing our brave bandana into shreds. Apollo's archery followed close behind. A hundred million rain-drop arrows he shot into our faces and drove through our flapping clothes. Back and forth, over us, under us, the great chariots rumbled.

We grew wetter, colder, more miserable. To leave our little shelter and try to stand against the on-slaught would be cruel punishment; to remain, with the icy water pouring in gullies over us, was just as cruel. The dilemma was abruptly solved by an

especially furious assault of the wind, which, accompanied by a cloud-burst, flung itself with a roar
against our battlement and toppled it precipitately on
to our heads.

I gave myself up for dead. I hoped I was dead;
anything to escape the unendurable plagues of cold
and rain. I lay stiff and aching under my granite
grave, until I heard Lazarus, somewhere in the mêlée
of arms and legs and stones, shout some terrible
blasphemy at the elements. Here was the old fighting
spirit! Rod and I joined in the chorus and supple-
mented Lazarus' profane-sounding vituperations
with a fine string of our own.

This castigation of the gods only increased their
indignation. It rained harder than ever. I do not
believe Jupiter would have let us live through one
more hour of this exposure had I not thought of a
perfectly obvious method of gaining relief from his
wrath—sacrifices! How *stupid* of us not to have
thought of this even before beginning the ascent. No
wonder he misunderstood our intentions. A ram
offered up that morning at our hillside camp would
undoubtedly have assured us bright skies and a clear
picture of the classic world from Olympus' top.
While we had carelessly forgotten to bring along up
the precipice any fat rams or wreath-hung bullocks,
it might not yet be too late for some modest offering
of propitiation.

Quickly I made an inventory of all our sacrificial properties, and in the torrential darkness commandeered whatever was disclosed. I should have liked to sacrifice Roderic's mustache, but it was undetachable. With this great prize eliminated, the collection was not very impressive. It consisted of one pocketful of sour, weather-beaten goat's cheese (from Lazarus), and a small bottle of *mastika,* a highly alcoholic Greek liquor which tastes so much like stale paregoric that even though it had been given to me by the shepherds for just such emergencies as this I would rather have frozen to death than drunk it. This *mastika* would be a splendid gift to Jupiter—since I couldn't swallow the awful poison anyway.

We were sorely handicapped by not knowing much about classic sacrificial ritual. Burning the offering on pyres was one way, but with our cheese dissolved to a soupy consistency, and with our matches floating around in our pockets, and nothing but dripping granite for fuel, we gave up *that* plan.

There was only one thing left to do,—drop the irresistible gifts solemnly into the abyss.

Overboard went the cheese, and as the *mastika* was poured after it, I suggested to Jupiter that he take note of our homage sufficiently to call off this damned shower-bath.

And would you believe it?—not fifteen minutes afterward, the rain desisted; the Thunderer's chariot

rumbled away over Thessaly; the cloud cavalry drew
aside its evil veil, and there, hanging radiantly in the
southern sky, the moon that we had seen at the
shepherds' spring the night before, smiled again.

Even so, though the rain had lasted hardly more
than an hour, we still had six or seven hours more to
endure our sodden clothes.  It wasn't nearly so bad,
though, now that we could see one another, and know
that we were free of any further persecution from the
gods.  Rod began to renew his interest in Venus, and
to regret that after all we had gone through
his grooming probably wouldn't be as *chic* as he'd like
to have it if she happened to return home in the morning to look him over.

A thousand years more passed, and then upon the
eastern heavens, far out over the Ægean, a gray light
grew.  Land and ocean began to unfold.  Before
Aurora's radiance, Diana waned, and drooped, and
sank to sleep, and left her rival in undisputed possession of the Grecian world.

In the startling glory of the sunrise, Roderic
and Lazarus and I almost forgot our frozen limbs,
and failed to notice one another's weary faces.  It
was just as well, for I'm sure our appearances and
expressions must have been not far removed from that
of three half-drowned alley-cats.  Even these poor
creatures would have forgotten their misery when the
chariot of the Sun drawn by his glowing horses not

rose but exploded from the sea, scattering golden fire against the defiant walls of Mount Olympus.

As the sun climbed upward into the storm-cleared sky we found ourselves pinnacled in a range of peaks,—all, all Olympus. From the foot of this throne of god all classic Greece rolled away, to Pelion and Ossa, to the plains of Thessaly, and the Vale of Tempe, to Mount Parnassus capped with snow, and the eternal isles of the Ægean. The valley toward the north opened toward Macedonia and Thrace. This valley was once the home of the Centaurs, and the happy land where Orpheus enchanted all nature with his music. Toward the west we saw the pass of Pitra through which the Persian barbarians under Xerxes, having crossed the Hellespont on a bridge of boats, invaded Greece to fight the battle of Thermopylæ. To the south was Thermopylæ itself, and far, far across the eastern ocean—but no farther than the gods could see—the walls of Troy!

What exultation danced within me! The afternoon before, Greece had been only an ocean of clouds, and veiled Olympus just one more mountain. Now, in all its splendor, I could see what I had come to see,—the Greece of myth and legend, of heroic deeds and godlike men, of Achilles and Ulysses, of Zeus and Athena, the immortal Greece of Homer's epic poetry, all beheld from the sacrosanct summit of Mount Olympus,—"Olympus, where the dwelling of the gods standeth fast forever."

The sun was well up now, and as we looked out
upon it, drinking in its life-giving glow, an eagle
came flying toward us from over the abyss. Nearer
and nearer he drew until we could mark his beak and
claws. Then just as the great bird on outstretched
wings sailed above our heads, he glanced down at us,
gave one vigorous scream and flew on. I confided
in Roderic that I believed the eagle was Zeus in
feathery form returning to investigate his invaded
habitation. I wanted so much to call him back and
further explain our position. I wanted to express
my appreciation for his gracious reception of our
sacrifice. But my wish was only vanity—he was
gone.

Roderic was painfully bored with my childish
idea about the eagle, and said my mind must be a bit
touched from the ordeal of the night before. He
assured me the eagle was only a grouchy bird, and my
god-infested Olympus only a high and barren hill.
He even claimed that the rain had already all but
stopped before I made the sacrifices. It was ap-
parent Roderic had become very cynical since
Venus had failed to show up. In fact he admitted
that so far as *he* was concerned the Greek gods were
a complete flop.

Yet even if he were right and rid of all illusions,
and even if I were only inspired by crazy dreams to
crazier action, was I not the richer of the two for hav-

ng indulged myself in the poetic notions of that fine old Greek god faith? Its fancy, its grace, its lyrical appeal, that had their haunts in shaded dale, or piny mountain, in the sea and the running brooks, these things the rationalists can not know or love. They have their faith of reason, but their hearts still have no language. Their civilization cast down the gods of Greece, and ever since, in cultural darkness, on hands and knees it seeks the shattered torch of Beauty and Humanity that from the lighthouse of Olympus illumined once the Western World.

# SYLVANIA

# CHAPTER III

RODERIC and I came down from Olympus feeling more encouraged than ever about our *Odyssey* expedition. So far as I was concerned, I felt it was a great stroke to have brought ourselves to Jupiter's attention right in the beginning, and to have impressed him with the fact that we were not impudent iconoclasts but pilgrims acknowledging his omnipotence and seeking his favors for our classic undertaking. It was far better to have had it out with him—thunderbolts and all—because now there would be no misunderstanding. We could go blithely ahead with our plans, knowing that our freezing and fighting and sacrificing on top the sacred mountain had not been in vain.

However, even Jupiter had no power over the Fates. With all his patronage we were not safe from disaster had it been so foreordained. And nobody in the world could advise us in regard to this matter of destiny except the oracle at Delphi. So we determined as our next move to consult this omniscient

prophet of Apollo, realizing it would be sheer folly—
and certainly most unclassic—not to. No ancient
Greek would ever have been so injudicious.

Once the idea became a definite plan, we began
to prepare for this new pilgrimage.

Pilgrims to the sacred shrine, we realized, should
always take along a few offerings. Rod and I looked
about for suitable gifts. We had our cameras,—but
were out of films. We had a box of expensive French
soap brought all the way from Paris and used only
on grand occasions,—but soap is rather a dangerous
thing to give sensitive people. We had our safety
razors,—but the oracle was a lady. The outlook was
most discouraging till I recalled that the oracle was
always crowned with a wreath of laurel, sacred to
Apollo, from the Vale of Tempe, his favorite haunt,
and that a fresh supply of these symbolic branches
might be very welcome. They would undoubtedly be
safer than soap,—and the Vale of Tempe lay right
in our path. I had been hoping to go there anyway
for a long time to investigate the rumors I'd heard
about this place being the chief rendezvous for the
sylvan deities of Greek mythology. More than anything in the world I wanted to meet a wood-nymph
face to face; and here was my chance.

On reaching this deity-inhabited locality, right at
the foot of Mount Olympus, we shook off our train
of unethereal gendarmerie who in passing sport shot

at every flying bird and furtive animal. We feared
they might by chance kill a hamadryad, or even shoot
Diana.

Our coats, our hats, our simple baggage, we en-
trusted to the departing militia to safeguard for us
in Larissa. In return we unburdened them of all
their food supplies, and two of their army rifles.
Thus fortified against any attack from man or nature,
we moved one morning at daybreak upon the Happy
Valley—the valley that the poets since the time of
Homer have populated with fauns and nymphs and
satyrs.

Our roadway led along the ancient route cut in
the living rock. Beside us the little Peneios River
flowed through deep shadows beneath the laurel
branches. Mount Olympus overhung the western
bank; the peaks of Ossa guarded the east. Sweeping
higher and still higher, these mighty walls rose far
above us, shattered into cliffs and towers whose
pinnacles just caught the first rays of sunshine. The
early hour, the dense tree canopy gave the green
gulfs through which we passed a gray mysterious
light. The grotesque plane-trees with their twisted
arms and Argus-eyes trailed into the gliding stream
to slake their morning thirst. Singing their
rhapsodies, all the birds of the universe, it seemed, had
sought this valley. Thrushes and swallows fluttered
their brown feathers in the shallow pools, and a flash

of yellow or a ruby streak told where an oriole had passed, or a blackbird with red wings.

How cool and calm and beckoning the morning river looked! We found a little strand of sand, put away our simple clothes, dropped into a pool of re-flected sky and floated idly with the clouds. We had not swum down-stream a hundred yards, when a babble of small bells, moving through the trees toward the river, began to come to us. I listened hopefully.

"Roderic," I said in subdued tones to my com-panion who was swimming leisurely beside me, "hear those bells? I'll bet that's Bacchus and his crew carousing through the woods."

"I'll bet it isn't," he replied as dryly as it was possible to reply with only his head and heels sticking out of the water.

"Well, I'm going to see, if you'll give me a chance and stop that noisy splashing," I said, crawling up on the rocks.

"I'll stop if you'll promise to bring me back an inebriated nymph with green eyes and red hair."

Promising that I would, and moving furtively lest I be observed myself, I crept along the bank, expecting any moment to catch sight of the lascivious old Sileni and the noisy satyr chorus dancing by in their perpetual festival of wine. But Bacchus saw me first, and, resenting the profanation of human presence, waved his twisted vine-wreathed wand through the air. Instantly he turned himself by magic into a shepherd boy, and all his rowdy followers into *goats*. I peeped through the branches, one second too late. Nothing remained of the bacchanalian revelers but the mingled musical bells. I could have wept from disappointment; perhaps I should have, had the entire parade of metamorphosed goats not moved in a solid body straight upon the spot where our clothes had been left lying on the bank, and thus made me forget all my chagrin in the face of this *much* more important crisis. Entirely ignoring the fact that the herd of bearded animals had just been sylvan demi-dieties, and recalling only the Capricornian propensity for linen and leather, I put all modesty aside and dashed in among them with bloodcurdling shouts to the heroic rescue of our pants. Bacchus shook his crook at me savagely and called down the wrath of all the Olympians on my head. I expected to be turned into a pig or wild-dog any moment by the outraged god, but I reasoned that this would not be so bad as our having to wander about Greece—Arcadian Greece though it was—wearing an inadequate coat of sunburn and a smile.

# WE CHARGE PARNASSUS

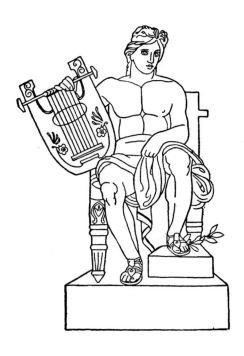

# CHAPTER IV

## WE CHARGE PARNASSUS

BACK at Larissa with our laurel offering, we took a motor-car next morning for Parnassus, and watched this sacred mountain grow in grandeur as we sped across the plains of Thessaly,—on to Delphi which lay upon the mountain's southern slopes.

The celebrated shrine is situated eighteen hundred feet above the Gulf of Corinth, on the side of a wild spectacular gorge that in itself fills one with awe, and reverence for the gods. Our motor ground up the steep slopes of the rocky canyon and deposited us at the hotel. At once we hurried out to the holy precinct, knowing, of course, that the oracle had been dumb for twenty centuries, and that the shrine was only a field of prostrate ruins; yet still believing that in a place of such dramatic associations, there must be adventure awaiting two faithful pilgrims like ourselves who came bearing fresh laurel wreaths from Tempe. Anyway we had determined that such a small obstacle as lack of a prophet was not going to interfere with our purpose. Having put so much store by this visit we were going to consult *an* oracle if not *the* oracle.

Reaching the sanctuary, we inquired where the vapor crevice was. Legend has it that goats browsing on these Delphian slopes of Mount Parnassus were thrown into convulsions when they approached a certain deep cleft in the side of the mountain, from which a peculiar intoxicating gas arose. The goatherd on inhaling it was affected in the same manner as the goats. The local inhabitants imputed the convulsive ravings, to which he gave utterance under the power of the exhalation, to Apollo's divine inspiration,—and a temple was straightway raised on the spot. I felt that if the vapor could hypnotize goats and goatherds it could do as much for Roderic, so we decided to seek the crevice, over which he agreed, grumblingly, to sit and breathe deeply of the Apollonian chlorine.

To our complete disappointment we learned there was no longer any crevice, nor any mystic vapor. How annoying! We must find a substitute. The hotel bar offered possibilities, but it was a problem to know which alcoholic aroma would have just the proper degree of intoxication on Oracle Roderic. Scotch whisky might stimulate beyond the point of receptivity; champagne might incline the prophet to rash and over-optimistic promises; certainly the dreadful native Greek *mastika* would never inspire anybody to foretell anything but death and disaster. I'd never want my fortune told with *that*. And then we opened a beer bottle. Instantly I knew we had found the correct asphyxiator. Rod's eyes took on a glazed far-away expression. He began to laugh softly. I jerked the potent bottle away from him, since it would never do to go into the mesmeric trance in the hotel bar. People might misunderstand.

Residing in our hotel at the time was an arresting young English poet who was so highly amused at our oracular efforts that we decided to give him a leading rôle in the ceremony. In ancient times there was always a consecrated priest who interpreted the oracle's mumblings, and Mr. William Watson Wright could play the priest's part to perfection, as he had the most gorgeous pink beard that ever adorned a pallid white face. Roderic was more than agreeable for this assistance since he was foreseeing some difficulty, even with the divine inspiration, in putting his prophecies into the customary iambic verse upon which I insisted.

Our priest was well informed on Delphic ritual. It would not be possible, he said, for the oracle to become the purveyor of divine auguries without first seeking absolution from all earthly contamination in the sacred Castalian fountain which gushed out of the rocks near by from beneath a great hewn-stone altar. The water was like ice, and Roderic demurred

from immersion in such an Arctic bath. So we com-
promised on a sprinkling baptism. I managed to get
enough water down his back, however, to cleanse
away a good part of his iniquities. He squirmed and
quarreled, but when I reminded him how countless
his sins were, he accepted the purification more gracefully.

I was thoroughly enjoying my rôle of purifier
when the priest announced that all Delphic pilgrims,
as well as prophets, had to purge themselves in this
same magic spring before consulting the oracle.
Roderic joyfully agreed with him and revenged himself by giving me as thorough a drenching in holy
water as I had given him. We then decided the
priest was not going to escape, and although he
strenuously insisted that Delphic dignitaries were already sacred and needed no further cleansing, we
determined to make an exception of him. And so,
breaking all precedent, we gave the immaculate Mr.
William Watson Wright the most violent purification
ever applied in the long history of the Castalian
spring.

Thus prepared to receive Apollo's divinations we
sought the Rock of the Sibyl, where, although there
were no noxious vapors, there was at least a crevice.
The laurel we had been saving for this very moment
was now brought forward, and, while it refused to
bend into a crown for the prophet's head, I managed

to balance a nice sprig fetchingly over one ear. Everything was set now for the administration of the beer-bottle afflatus.

The priest drew out the cork and rested the gas-tank on the rock beneath Rod's nose. Once more he breathed the celestial ether; once more he seemed to be transported to another, fairer land. Priest William now told me to put my question.

"Will my Odyssey be a success?" I asked reverently. "Shall I get safely to Troy, and then hold fast to Ulysses' trail? Will the gods blow me home for Christmas, or will Neptune persecute me and keep me ten years from Penelope?"

The interpreter turned to the laureled oracle and repeated my question. The prophet took several more deep inhalations from the malty depths and began to mutter the reply. The priest clutched his pink beard tensely, and, putting his ear close to the entranced clairvoyant, slowly translated, extemporaneously, the holy gibberish:

"The — shade — of — dead — Ulysses — on —
    your — undertaking — smiles.
  You'll — meet — with — many — labors — set —
    against — you — by — great — Zeus.
But — through — your — comrade's — brav'ry —
    you'll — escape — from — all — the — guiles
Of — Circe — and — the Sirens — if ————
    Rod Crane's — advice — you'll — use."

This oracle business wasn't so bad after all. I decided to ask another question that was troubling me:

"Shall I ever be recognized as a writer?"

Once more the prophet breathed deeply from the supernal flask:

"You — must — conquer — Mount — Parnassus —
    if — to — fame — you — would — aspire,
And — from — its — highest — summit, — as —
    the — sun — bursts — from — the — sea,
Invoke — the — god — Apollo — for — his —liter-
    ary — fire.
But — even — then — the — prophet, — if — you —
    want — *his* — frank — opinion,
Believes — that — wholesale — groceries — are —
    truly — your — dominion."

"Tell the oracle *his* opinion is not required," I retorted. "'Also tell him that he's not yet answered my question, and that if he will give me a favorable reply I'll pay his hotel bill." (In ancient times a bribe was known to have influenced the divine responses more than once.) Our hotel expenditures would cover two days or more. The offer had instant effect:

"If — these, — my — words — of — wisdom, —
    on to — paper — you — will — write,
A — hundred — thousand — people — in —your —
    story — will —delight."

Ah, worthy oracle! Wise Apollo! This inspired medium had now best be disenchanted quickly lest he also ask for his railroad fare and change his mind about my literary future. The holy incense was removed; the prophet's vision came back to Delphi; the priest let go his flaming beard. We called the ceremony to a close and adjourned to the hotel.

As we walked back, the oracle's first sincere response to my inquiry relating to my literary career, kept ringing in my ears: "You must conquer Mount Parnassus, if to fame you would aspire, and invoke the god Apollo for his literary fire, as the sun bursts from the sea." Roderic and I with Olympus only three days behind us had had enough mountain-scaling for a while, but with the oracle offering this one and only hope of fulfilling my aspirations, I must charge Parnassus—and at once. So in an hour we were off up the eighty-two-hundred-foot slope of this great symbolic mountain that has been sacred from time immemorial to Apollo and the muses.

All day long, from eleven in the morning till sundown we pressed upward as fast as our guide and pack-horse could walk, through cool murmuring pine woods, across little flat plateaux, past the famous Korykian Grotto where the most notorious Bacchic festivals of antiquity were celebrated, reaching the higher slopes covered with huge tumbled blocks of jagged stones around and over which we had to pick our way with the utmost care.

The sun was low in the west before we arrived at the ruined chalet in a little valley some thousand feet below the summit. Here we spent the night. How luxurious a fire and shelter seemed in comparison with the ordeal on top Olympus! At four in the morning we moved on up the last great dome in ample time to reach the top before sunrise, and dropped upon the summit boulder to recover our labored breath.

Every moment now the light grew brighter, and disclosed more distant miles. Olympus, and Ossa, and Pelion, to the north, thrust their summits through the mist. To the south, the Gulf of Corinth opened at our feet, and the Peloponnesus spread beyond.

Any further inspection of the landscape was cut short by the sun's imminent arrival. It was just on the point of rising out of Skyros, one of the far Ægean isles. Hurriedly I made ready to pray to Apollo, in keeping with the oracle's bidding, "as the sun bursts from the sea." Here it came—a great glow diademed the rocky island—brighter—clearer— with a shower of light it broke through the horizon.

"O great Apollo, god of poetry, thou who walkest over the mountains and the waves, leaving thy robe upon the ocean foam, thou god of harmony, thou inspiration to music and to art, hear my prayer. Grant unto me but one of thy thousand sunbeam shafts with which thou kindlest the creative fires.

Guide me and encourage me with thy light. Let me be touched by thy grace, that I may see clearly, and follow only, in the songs I wish to sing, that which is true, and beautiful, and enduring—"

"—and, dear Apollo,"—Roderic, praying vigorously alongside, interrupted my invocation by speaking right out loud—"please bless mama and papa, and make me a good little boy, forever and ever, Amen!"

# ACROPOLITIS

# CHAPTER V

THE bluest waves I've ever seen sped past as our coastal steamer from Delphi crossed the sunlit Gulf of Ægina. The Island of Salamis rose abruptly on our left. We rounded a small promontory and steered straight for the mainland that now loomed ahead. Roderic, leaning over the rail beside me, suddenly gripped my arm, and raising his hand with a dramatic gesture, pointed to ——

I saw it! A surge of rapture swept through me. There before us, painted against a violet veil of mountains a league or two from the sea, lifting high into the air its temple-crowned rock-altar, spread beneath its halo of immortality, gleamed the most radiant, the most delicate, the most sacred shrine we were to find in all our pilgrimage—ATHENS!

A single beam of sunlight, pouring through the flocks of clouds that roamed across the Attic plain, fell like a searchlight on the Acropolis. Enthroned upon its crest, the far-famed Parthenon, haggard but still majestic in its columned splendor, sprang forth from the shadows, the crown of glory set upon the brow of this queen of classic capitals.

That evening as Roderic and I dined in the shadow of the Acropolis, rising black and sheer against the stars, I thought: "How beautiful it would be, on such a lovely night as this, to climb up to the battlements of that high pinnacle and look out upon the mountains and the sea!" I knew the waning moon would rise, perhaps two hours later, the same moon that, full, had shone so brightly several nights before on Mount Olympus. I had also learned in advance that the Acropolis was open to the public for three nights each lunar month when the moon was at its zenith. But by three days we had missed this period of dispensation. That afternoon, the Acropolis gate, as usual, had been made fast at sunset, and two thousand years ago the Acropolis walls had been made proof against just such invaders as myself.

"Remember the Persians," whispered Temptation. "They found a secret stairway. Perhaps it's still there."

"But it's so dark—you'll break your neck scrambling up those rocks," admonished Discretion.

"Then take matches, fool!" was the sharp retort.

I took matches, my own and all of Roderic's, since he was too busy getting us settled at the hotel to want to accompany me on any marauding expedition.

our first night in Athens, and on second thought, while the *maître d'hôtel* wasn't looking, seized the pink candle from our table.  As I bade my companion good-by, it was agreed that if I did not return before dawn he would mount to the Acropolis next morning as soon as the gates were open, and join me in order that we might see the Parthenon together by sunlight. Then I moved forward to the grand assault, sparkling inside that such a noble and novel adventure was still left on earth.  My complete ignorance of the citadel's vulnerable points, of the distribution of night watchmen, of any helpful information whatsoever, made the expedition all the more alluringly hazardous.  I would have an opportunity of finding out all these things for myself.

It was obvious, even as I climbed the encircling highroad to the Acropolis gates, that the eastern and southern walls were eliminated.  They towered straight up above me, sheer and naked.  Perhaps the western end, containing the formal entrance, would be less hostile to my plans.

As anticipated, I found the bronze grill doors immovably locked, and there was no climbing over them, for they were only indentations in a great marble surface.  I whistled enticingly for the night watchman, prepared to force the entrance with drachmas.  Only Echo heard my notes.  I could look through the grill, straight up the broad marble steps that led beneath the Doric colonnade of the beautiful Propylæa, the monumental gateway which rose above me, pale and mysterious in the starlight "like a brilliant jewel on the front of Athens' coronet." This glimpse into the forbidden sanctuary only fired anew my eagerness to reach the Parthenon. I wanted to bend asunder the cursed bronze bars and beat them nto submission. But only trinitrotoluene could have done that.

Casting about impatiently for new routes, I observed a rocky terrace to the right, and, crawling up this with the aid of my walking cane, I saw that it continued in the form of a ledge, at a not unscalable angle, on up the foundation of the charming little temple of the Wingless Victory. In my enthusiasm over the finding of this steep but adequate rock ladder, I clambered along it with such careless haste that a shelf of loose gravel was dislodged. Rattling noisily down the slope it crashed on to the tin roof of a modern cottage, the home of an Acropolis warden, which, because of the darkness, I had not even noticed. Instantly a half-dozen huge watch-dogs came bounding out of nowhere and in a savage chorus announced to all Attica that I was trying to steal the Parthenon. The warden rushed after them, jabbering and storming and gesticulating. While it was all unintelligible to me, I supposed he meant "Come down."

Smarting from the humiliation, I turned to the left

side of the entrance pylon, to see what the northern
slopes had to offer.  In a moment I realized this was
the weak link of the fortification.  The rocks were
creviced and caverned, and unguarded by any Acro-
polean hell-hounds.  Before I had gone a hundred
yards, I came by chance, in a small hollowed-out cave
used for a chapel, upon the famous Klepsydra spring
from which, though it is now isolated outside the walls,
the Acropolis garrisons in classic times drew their
water.

I continued my scramble, in and out, over and
under the topographical confusion, and presently
found myself before the mouth of a grotto.  Grateful
for my pink candle, I lighted the poor little thing, and
plunged into the abysmal blackness of the interior.
Here, surely, I would find the secret stairway.  But
each fissure of the grotto ended in a blank wall.  I
was only in the ancient shrine of Pan—a shrine dedicated to the pastoral god in tribute to the assistance
he lent the Athenians in the battle of Marathon.  The
dark and twisted cavern rocks cast such a weird
reflection, the light of the flickering candle was so
ghostly, I thought once or twice I saw the grinning
old goat-foot seated in the shadows, ready to make
my blood run cold with some mischievous snort.  But
of secret steps there was none.

Back in the open once more, I found a faint path,
and followed it hopefully.  It led straight up to a

deep artificial breach in the cliff face which obviously
had once been a sort of postern gate to the Acropolis.
The entrance this time was closed by a thin wall made
of wooden frames covered with tin, four feet broad
and twenty feet high. Where this wall joined the
rock-facing there was a perfect ladder of cracks and
crevices up which any normally agile person could
climb with perfect ease. It was but a moment's effort
to reach the top of the obstruction, and descend by
means of the horizontal cross-strips of the frame that
braced the back. Twenty ancient hewn steps led up
to the surface of the plateau. The Acropolis guar-
dians had locked the front door with a thousand locks,
built a great wall around, and left the back door open.

The Persian leader who secretly gained access to
this stoutly defended fortress by some such entrance
as the one I had found, never raised his head above
the rocky floor more stealthily than I, nor set foot
upon it with a faster-beating heart. Yet how different were the consequences of our similar strategy.
*He* met the surprised garrison and dragged them
away into slavery. *I* met the starlit Parthenon, and
before a blow was struck, surrendered unconditionally
to its grim and time-worn beauty.

I was not a minute too soon. From the sharp
black crest of Mount Hymettus a glow as from a
burning forest was lighting the night. It was the
late-rising moon. Entranced by its dramatic ap-

proach I stood motionless, waiting, almost breathlessly, for its silver flash to peep above the
ridge. Straight out of the historic mountaintop it
sailed—a rim—a half—and then the glowing oval goddess revealed herself completely, kissed Hymettus'
crest good-by and mounted upward, smiling gently
upon an enchanted world.

Only then did I look back at the Parthenon. It
rose in ghost-like majesty from amid a sea of fragments,—not a misty distant ruin as seen from Salamis; no longer an elusive obscure phantom illumined
by the stars, but a real and radiant temple come to
life. One moment had worked a magic change. The
pain and sadness had disappeared from its desolate
face. The majestic marble colonnades, stained by
the sunshine of two thousand years, beaten by the
summer's wind and by the winter's rain, had turned
to alabaster and to pearl. My heart-beat quickened
before such heroic harmony,—moonlight and marble,
serene and eternal. The prostrate columns, the
shattered capitals took shape and line and color. My
fancy saw them back in place, gracing over every
scar. Once more the statues ranged along the porti-
cos; the gods returned from exile and took their places
on the pediments. An Athenean procession with
garlands and music moved up the marble stairs to do
honor to Athena for some well-earned victory. In
imagery the Golden Age of Pericles lived again.

Into this throng of worshipers I too must go; into the temple.  Bending low, moving forward noiselessly, clinging to the shadows of block and battlement, watching for the figures of night watchmen, I crept toward the Parthenon.  The massive steps were attained.  A moving, half-veiled shadow, I climbed them one by one, and, unchallenged, reached the refuge of the marble forest.

What loveliness rose all about me!  Broadside against my colonnade the moonlight streamed, leaving a swath of silver, then of shadow, then of silver, then of shadow, down the lofty aisles.  On across the gleaming flagstones I slipped on tiptoe.  The cella wall toward the sea inside the portico was shattered, leaving receding stumps of marble that climbed like a gigantic stairway to the cornices.  On hands and knees I pulled myself up these huge blocks until I reached the crowning stone, and could stand and look back upon the enchanted picture.

Never have I faced a scene that stirred my very soul as deeply as this picture of the brooding broken Parthenon spread below me in the moonlight.  The sight of its haggard marble, its butchered glory, made me faint and weak within.  A lump of bitterness filled my throat, and a rage swept over me against the Venetian vandals who had wantonly gutted this sublime Palace of Art.

With all its prostration, the Parthenon is still

the most overpowering ruin on earth—overpowering not from magnitude or richness, but because of its serene and classic perfection of form. Its terrible beauty is intellectual, not sensual. It was reared to glorify Athena, the Goddess of *Wisdom*. It was the ideal of intelligence supreme expressed in marble. From cold stone, the artistic giants who built the Parthenon embodied the spirit of the "Greek Fire" that has civilized the world. In Pentelic marble they wrought this immortal monument to the Greek passion for Knowledge, for Culture and for Freedom. In this moonlit temple spreading in silver shades below me, I beheld "the supreme effort of genius in the pursuit of beauty," the triumph of the ideal by which men once were able to become like gods.

But beware—what was that hollow sound? A night guard with a lantern emerged from nowhere and glided along the portico. No harm would come to me were my presence detected. I should only be expelled! . . . so I stopped breathing till he got away. Then cautiously I crept down the stair-stepped wall-end and looked about for new delights.

One need not look far in the Acropolis, since every time-worn block has beauty and every inch of it has memories. The spirits of "half the immortalities of earth" haunt this hallowed scene. Here Pericles stood, there Phidias trod; here Socrates taught philosophy to young Plato, there Alexander the

Great piled his captured shields. I scarcely knew which way to turn. In the dilemma my eye caught sight, a hundred yards away, of the exquisite little "Porch of the Maidens," one of the most delicate and beautiful creations of a supremely artistic age. The portico roof is supported not by columns but by six figures of marble maidens,—and oh, what lovely, gentle, life-like maids they are, standing there so easily, so reposed, with slightly bended knee, and carrying the simple architrave on their graceful heads as if it were the most agreeable duty in the world! The diaphanous draperies ripple in soft and supple folds from their young breasts. Their marble hair waves tenderly about their mobile faces. The moon, still in her search for beauty, had climbed to just that fortunate corner of the sky where her beams could fall luxuriously upon these enchanted maidens, nor yet reveal the black recess behind, so that they floated, pale and pearl and phantom-like, against a curtain of dark velvet. The beauty-seeking moon seemed to know that here, at last, she had found beauty, and to linger with this long-sought prize, pouring out upon their faces all her radiant benediction.

In a deep-shadowed corner of the portico I found a smooth broad step, and stopped to worship a moment at the feet of the ghostly maidens. How sweet it was to relax amid such loveliness! In the intensity of the day I had not thought to rest, but now a dreamy

lassitude came over me, and I half forgot the world.
The breeze from Mount Hymettus, blowing like a
soft caress, whispered songs of bees and pine trees'
murmurings. All the earth, outside my shadow, was
gowned in silver mystery. Touched by its hypnotic
spell I drifted with the moonlight into half-haunted
dreams, and thought I heard a marble maiden—
speak:

"There's a stranger lying on the steps, Persephone."

I listened—it was the corner figure.

"A strange hour for visitors; I wonder what he's
doing here?"

"It must be to sleep. He hasn't moved for half
an hour."

"But I'm *not* asleep," I blurted out, moving
around the corner to where I could come closer,—and
immediately hated myself for fear I might have disenchanted them.

"Well, what then *are* you doing?"—how relieved
I felt!

"I mean no harm; I slipped up the steps on the
north side to pay homage to your moonlit loveliness."

"Oh, I see," said the corner figure. "But I didn't
know that route was open."

"It most certainly isn't," I answered with a
laugh. "It's blocked by a tin wall. I had to crawl
over it like a lizard."

"Please don't say *lizard*," she exclaimed. "They've been creeping over us for two thousand summers, and we detest the name."

"*Two thousand summers!*" I gasped. "And I thought you were not a day over eighteen."

"Oh, but we're immortal."

"Have you names?" I asked hesitatingly.

"Why certainly. I'm Philomela."

"And I'm Persephone," said her neighbor.

"And you?" I asked, looking at the third figure.

"Oh, she's dead," said Philomela sadly. "Flora used to stand there, until Lord Elgin carried her away long ago. Somebody put back a substitute—but she's only terra-cotta. Electra is on the other corner. Cyrene stands behind her, and Thalia's behind me. Have you a name?"

"Yes." I told her what it was. "Not very classic, is it? I live in America."

"America——? I never heard of it. Is it as far away as Thrace?"

I gasped again. "No-o. Hardly as far as that."

"Why have you come to Athens?"

"Well, you see I'm retraveling Homer's *Odyssey*. I climbed Mount Olympus recently to propitiate the gods, and then came here on my way to Troy."

"You climbed Mount *Olympus!*" exclaimed Philomela. "What desecration! Father Zeus should have hit you with a thunderbolt."

"He tried to," I explained, "only I dodged. But enough about me. What brought *you* to Athens?"

"Why, we were hewn out of Mount Pentelicus and set up here during the Golden Age, as part of the temple to mark the spot where Athena strove with Poseidon for the possession of the city."

"Who won?" I asked simply.

*"Who won!"* exclaimed Philomela. "What *stupidity!* Athena won of course and became the patron goddess of Athens. The whole Acropolis is dedicated to her."

"Were you here when the Persians came?" I asked, trying to change the subject.

"Oh no. We just missed that, fortunately. We've heard all about it, though. That must have been a dreadful time. Only a few hundred helpless people who couldn't go with Themistocles and his fighters to Salamis barricaded themselves here. Xerxes and his entire army attacked the Acropolis, but you see how strong it is. The poor little garrison might have held fast till the Greeks came back from the sea-fight, if some traitor hadn't shown the Persians the secret entrance. The garrison was surprised and easily overcome, and every standing stone on the Acropolis was leveled to the ground.

"We missed all that, as I say. Still, we have had enough tragedy since. It's been nothing but heartbreaks and violence all our lives. We were sculptured

during the great war with Sparta,—under the most
trying circumstances.  We've been hurled to earth
more than once.  You see we've lost our arms and
noses; it's only a miracle we stand here at all.  The
Romans left *us* intact even though they did carry
away hundreds of our neighbors.  Several times during the Byzantine period we were all but dragged to
Constantinople  to  enrich  some  Christian  church.
Why, our temple *was* a church for a thousand years.

"Bad as that was, it wasn't half so bad as the
Turks.  They made harem quarters out of us, and
stuck  a  minaret  up  beside  us.   And  then—the
Venetians"—I thought I saw Philomela's eyes fill
with tears—"they were fighting to dislodge the Turks
from the Acropolis.  One of their dreadful shells fell
into the Parthenon and exploded the powder mag-
azine stored there.  I'll never forget that terrible
moment if I live another two thousand years.  There
was a burst of fire; the Parthenon roof was blown
into the air—I saw it all—and almost half the columns were hurled down.  The explosion nearly
rocked us over too.  It was agony for a long time
after that,—all the sculpture on the Acropolis was
hacked and stolen by everybody.  Lord Elgin tore
Flora from us, and allowed our architrave to collapse.
Soon after the Turks pounded us with cannon for a
whole month, fighting with the Greeks in their War
of Independence.  That was the time our faces suf•

fered so. Now, we're well cared for,—now that it's
almost too late and we are disfigured and separated."

"Oh, my Philomela, you are still the loveliest, and
still the most admired little monument in all Greek
architecture," I said consolingly. "Remember, even
the moon, who has seen the beauty of every land,
seemed to stop in her course to-night to honor and
to brighten you. Think of me, immortal maiden, who
must grow old and perish, while you may drink the
sunshine of two thousand summers more, and come
to life on every moon-mad night like this. If I could
only stay and talk to you—I've never known an
ancient Greek before—how happy I would be! But
you see the night has passed—the moon is trembling
in the west—dawn will be here so soon—I must hide
back in the shadows before the watchman comes.
Here's a little blue flower I found beside the
Klepsydra Spring as I was looking for the secret
gate. Make it immortal like you, Philomela, so I
may never be forgotten. Good-by, Persephone—
good-by, Electra. I'll see Flora some day soon, and
I shall tell her you miss her, and need her, and love
her, eternally—good-by."

Sadly I crept away—back to my dark recess. I
had waited a moment too long, so enslaved was I by
the charm of the marble maidens. When I moved, the
dawning light had disclosed my presence to the
guards. I heard footsteps coming toward me; some

one touched my shoulder. I squeezed my eyes together lest I behold some ogreish night-watchman. But there was no escape. I screwed up my courage—and looked!

Everywhere was brilliant morning sunshine—and there, smiling quizzically down at me—stood *Roderick*

# MARATHON MADNESS

# CHAPTER VI

## MARATHON MADNESS

WE REMAINED in Athens almost a month. It is a most sociable city, even in July, and our frequent good intentions to leave behind its gaiety, and depart manfully on our Odyssean expedition, were always frustrated by an invitation to another tea party. Roderic, who generously did all the worrying for both of us and thus relieved me of that responsibility, woke up one Monday morning with what he thought was a neat way to conquer our irresolution.

"Dick, if you'll promise to get away from this demoralizing place with me next Wednesday, I'll give you a birthday luncheon to-morrow. We can invite everybody we know, clean up our social obligations, and tell them all good-by. Then we'll *have* to go."

"That sounds very fine, Mr. Crane; only to-morrow isn't my birthday,—it's six months off."

"I know it—we probably won't be together then, so let's celebrate now."

"I'll promise, on my honor, to go Wednesday, but

if you give me a birthday party to-morrow, I can't be there."

"Why not?"

"I've got to go to Marathon this afternoon, and can't get back in time."

"Why don't you go this morning and return to-night? There's motor service. I'll go with you."

"You don't understand, Rod. I'm going to run back. Would you want to do that too?"

He slid with a howl under the covers of his bed.

"Oh, stop groaning. Pheidippides' run from Marathon to Athens was one of the most romantic events in the record of athletic achievement. I'd rather run the Marathon over the actual original course than be president"—and then I added spitefully, since Rod was always berating my Democratic partisanship—"especially a Republican president."

"I wouldn't! Not in this August weather. Anyway I never heard of Pheidippides,—so he can't have been very important."

"He was probably the most important runner that ever lived."

"What was there at Marathon he was running away from?"

"Roderic, your ignorance is colossal,—and after a month in *Athens!* Cornell must be proud of you."

"Oh, I can't know everything."

"Well, I insist you get a guide-book to Greece,

and read about the most famous battle and most
heroic run in history."

"I haven't time.  You tell me—you know so much,
I'll order breakfast while you recite chapter one."

"Will you promise to keep your mind on what I'm
saying?"

"Yes, ma'am."

"Shall I speak with or without the gestures?"

"With."

And so, as we ate our rolls, and omelette, and
Hymettus honey, I undertook to enlighten my be-
nighted companion:

"If you had spent your time in college reading
the classics, as I did, instead of wasting it on those
depressing engineering books, you'd know that
Pheidippides was the fastest runner of ancient
Athens.  Great athletes were highly important people in those days, and often received public offices.
Pheidippides was made official messenger boy.  All
he had to do was run fifty miles or so every day to
Thebes or Corinth or Delphi to bear the thrilling
news that one of the elders—who probably had three
chins and wasn't an especially good runner himself—
had delivered a three-hour oration against the de-
cadence of the age or some other dull subject.  Of
course Pheidippides gave his services to the army
when the Persians set upon Greece in 490 B. C.  The
invaders landed at Marathon, only nineteen miles

from Athens, and the Greek army took the short-cut
over the mountains to block further approach. . . .
I think you might at least offer me a cigarette while
you're helping yourself to my package."

"But you can't do the gestures and smoke at the
same time, can you?"

"Don't be ridiculous. Of course I can. Give me
a light. Now—what was I saying?"

"Announcing a big fight between the Greeks and
the Armenians."

"Armenians! *Persians,* Dummkopf!"

"My mistake."

"The Persians had a quarter of a million soldiers
and the Athenians only ten thousand. One good
Athenian was equal to about ten anybody else, so
that made it nearly even. One of the fine points about
the battle—this will probably be over your head—was
that it settled the cultural destiny of our Western
World. Had the Persians won the battle an Asiatic
civilization would have been thrust upon Greece, and
it is entirely likely that Rome, which was a cultural
disciple of Athens, would in turn have given an
Oriental stamp to all Europe. But the gods were
not so inclined. They fired the Greeks with a valor
of desperation that sent the quarter-million invaders
flying for their boats."

"Do you expect me to believe that?"

"Well, if you don't believe my story it only proves

what I have always said,—that you have absolutely
no imagination. The handful of Athenians *did* defeat
the Persians, and civilization was saved, whether you
approve or not. The instant the invaders broke for
their ships a young Greek soldier was seen to throw
down his armor and run rapidly toward the mountain pass. It was Pheidippides. Athens must know.
Twenty-six miles to the city it was by the seacoast
route,—nineteen over the mountains. He chose the
shorter harder way. The trail led up a ravine and
over a rugged ridge. The whole Greek army had
passed along this route ten days before. Even then
it was still difficult for a runner.

"The summit of the pass was reached and the
down-hill pace begun. Instead of relaxing along
this easier road Pheidippides increased his speed.
Shepherds, knowing so hard pressed a runner from
Marathon must be bearing life-and-death news to
Athens, rushed to the roadside to make anxious in-
quiries. Pheidippides realized his breath was too
limited to spend here. These people were safe. It
was Athens that must know.

"The road now rounded the northern end of
Mount Pentelicus, and he could see the plains of
Attica—at least he could if this map you wasted fifty
drachmas on is any good—Attica, his homeland, safe
from the Persian sword and firebrand. Beautiful emo-
tions swelled up in the runner's heart. . . . If you

aren't going to eat your roll give it to me. My bread and honey refuse to come out even. Thanks. . . .

"In Athens a tense and ominous quiet had prevailed all day. Previous messengers had brought news that the dreaded battle had begun, and everybody walked around a bit nervously. Early that morning a neglected crippled youth had climbed laboriously to the Acropolis and posted himself on the highest stone he could find facing toward Marathon,—I think I know just where it is. He kept his sharp eyes glued to the thin white ribbon that led to the battle-field. Others were watching, but he saw it first,—a small cloud of dust rising from a tiny speck moving toward Athens. He rubbed his eyes to be sure. There was no mistaking it. A runner! A runner! His cry of discovery was echoed and repeated until it reached the market-place. Crowds began to stream out along the road to meet the messenger. He came on, black with sweat and dust. He did not attempt to speak or relax his pace. He reached the Rue de Kephisia and, followed by a swarm of people, plunged on to the market-place. He was reeling——" I stood up on the bed to act out the reels. "A hundred hands stretched forth to catch him—that way. Pheidippides had reached his goal. 'Victory,' he gasped out, and bit the dust quite dead,— just like this," I added, collapsing among the pillows.

Roderic patted his hands together in applause.

"Very good! Very good! But I'm glad it's over."

Two thousand four hundred and five years after the death of Pheidippides, I stood on the Marathon mound, with the mountains before me at the foot of which the Athenian army had camped, and, behind, the shore where the Persian fleet was drawn. I was alone, for Roderic, despite my eloquent story, had not been thrilled sufficiently to make the trip. Had I planned to run back along the highway he would have gone along in a motor to accompany me, but as I was determined to follow Pheidippides' own trail over the mountains, Rod's companionship—except on foot—was out of the question. And to walk nine- teen miles—much less run it—in this scorching weather, was Rod's idea of the last stages of imbecility.

Remaining behind, he proceeded to make all his plans for my birthday luncheon the following noon, and since I wasn't going to be there anyway, invited a lot of people I didn't know and several others I didn't like. He escorted me to the motor-bus and requested that if I was determined to imitate Phei- dippides, would I please omit the part where he falls dead,—it would be very discommoding to be left alone at this stage of our expedition.

On arrival at the village of Marathon at sundown, I could find no other sleeping quarters save on top the one table the one "restaurant" in the community boasted. However, my travel style on this occasion was in keeping with the accommodations, for I had left behind in Athens hat, coat, cane,—even my toothbrush. Anticipating the nineteen-mile run next day in midsummer heat I should also have left shirt and trousers had I not feared that perverse and narrow-minded convention would have me seized as a lunatic if I were caught galloping about Attica without them.

I couldn't sleep that night. There was something too dramatic in the air to allow me any peace. Of course to the local bovine inhabitants, the field of Marathon is only an immense and meaningless vine-yard producing a wine which they sell to greasy Athenian merchants for many drachmas, but to me Marathon was one of the soul-stirring corners of the world, and no place to sleep over.

Stumbling in the darkness upon restaurant chairs, saucepans and cats, I found the door, and stepped out about eleven o'clock into the starlit street. Not a person was to be seen. It was a village dead in slumber. The friendliest of the six dogs that also occupied my chamber begged to be allowed to take part in whatever mischief I was up to, and I gladly obliged him. Together we straggled out of the village toward the plain.

Finding a spur of the mountains that overlooked the sea and hemmed in one end of the battle-field, we climbed to the six-hundred-foot crest and reclined against a boulder to rest. Fido curled up by my side and straightway went to sleep,—with the immortal field of Marathon, the graves and ghosts of heroic Athenians, the strand that buried the bones of many a Persian,—all spreading out below for his particular inspection. Poor beast, he was no poet.

Summer nights in Attica are magic nights. The stars seem to know that it was once a sacred land, sacred no more, and in mourning for her departed majesty, they shine with ten thousand glistening tears upon the ruins of the glory that was Greece. They are no less bright now than that September night when over this same hallowed ground Miltiades roused his Athenians to hurl back on the morrow the Persian invaders who threatened to crush Greek liberty.

Looking out over the plain from my little mountaintop, I grieved a bit that Byron could not know what liberation had come since he stood here, a hundred years ago, mourning the Turkish bondage that ground down this classic land. "The mountains look on Marathon," now as then, "and Marathon looks on the sea;

"And musing there an hour alone,
I dream'd that Greece might still be free;
For standing on the Persians' grave,
I could not deem myself a slave."

How prophetic these verses seemed, and how I rejoiced that the poet's dream of Greek freedom for which he had given his strength, his fortune and his very life, had come to pass so abundantly.

Fido—and I wondered perhaps if one of the pup's ancestors accompanied Byron on *his* climb alone to this hillcrest—was awake and asking to go home. So back we strolled, beneath the stars, to our restaurant table-top.

At dawn, well provisioned for my solitary Marathon, I again left the village, and tramped the three miles to the twenty-four-hundred-year-old battle-field mound raised by the victorious Athenians in the center of the plain. It was here that runners from fifteen nations gathered in 1896 when the classic Olympic games were first revived, and raced to Athens by the longer route (the mountain trail used by Pheidippides being entirely impractical as a race course). To the sincere delight of every true athlete in the world, the event was won, properly, by a Greek.

Climbing to the fifty-foot summit of this hillock, I took a sweeping look around at sea and sky and mountain, "got set"—"on my mark"—and "went," just as my wrist watch struck six.

Before trotting a quarter-mile I began to have a vague suspicion that I was no Pheidippides. At Princeton with the New Jersey winter weather at zero, a five-mile jog over the frozen hills about Lake

Carnegie had been fine sport. But several years had passed since then, and with them all my claims to kinship with the antelope. Very shortly as the perspiration began to stream down my face, I decided that the nineteen miles to Athens, beneath the murderous midsummer sun, were going to damage me more than the five miles to Princeton Junction and back used to do.

Oh well, there was no hurry. I wasn't bearing tidings to a palpitating Athens that the Persians had been pushed off the front porch. The only things that awaited me were blistered heels and a suspicious scrutiny from the police, and neither of these incentives was worth running myself to death for like Pheidippides.

Thank heaven, there is such a thing as "second wind." By the time I had trotted the three-mile width of the plain from the mound to the site of the Greek encampment at the foot of the mountains, respiration was fairly well ordered, so that now I was really better prepared to meet the difficulties of the trail up the gorge than I should have been at the outset.

Along with the lack of a trousers-problem, Pheidippides had a big advantage over me in that this mountain path in his day was a principal route to Athens from Marathon, and in consequence well enough marked for ten thousand Athenian soldiers to march along it. I'd like to see them try it now. With the era of wheeled vehicles, the longer sea level route gained preference and the once proud mountain road was abandoned to the forest and the stream. This being the case, one of the ten good reasons I didn't break any records on my Marathon was because so much time was lost looking for the elusive wisp of a path, which had a way of disappearing beneath a rock or up a tree as fast as I found it again.

For the first hour my determination to imitate Pheidippides showed no signs of weakening. I was resolved to "tell Athens," though just what it was I was going to tell Athens, I'd not decided. However, after six or seven miles of sun and sticks and stones, faintness from lack of fuel began to discomfort me. So, on reaching the summit of the divide, I sat down in the shade to recover my breath. Disinterring a loaf of bread and a package of cheese I decided to postpone telling Athens till I'd had a rest and a meal. If Pheidippides had done likewise he might have lived to run another day.

By the time I had reached a point ten miles from the Marathon mound where the country had become fairly well settled, a tormenting thirst had seized me with such violence that I decided to sacrifice Athens and everybody in it to the Persians for one drink of water. A small refreshment shop in a hamlet I passed through offered itself and I leaped upon it.

There wasn't any water. Because of the prolonged drought every spring in the neighborhood had dried up. One of the shop attendants had gone to a reservoir some distance away to bring back a supply. He wouldn't return for half an hour;—there was wine. I had the proprietor hurriedly open his nearest decanter. It was vile, but of all the drinks I've drunk (in the words of Gunga Din) I'm gratefulest to one from this Greek bartender. Glass after glass was emptied. In fact so much wine disappeared that when I sought the road again it reeled about in the most amazing manner. I had to hold tight to keep from being thrown by it. Running was too redic'lous. I felt so jolly, just rolling along and stopping to tell everybody in English that everyshing was all right, since the Pershuns were in wild flight. They seemed delighted to hear the good news. I wanted to tarry and tell them all about the fight, but Ashens mush know; so I tripped blithely on, around the end of Mount Pentelicus, and there—stretching out toward the sea and wrapped in purple summer haze, the plains of Attica stood first on one end and then on the other,—Attica, safe from the Persian sword and firebrand. Wheeeee!!!

At Kephisia, twelve miles from Marathon and seven from the Acropolis, my enthusiasm to tell Ashens became so strong I hailed a taxicab, broke the glad tidings to the chauffeur and jumped in, beseeching him to hurry. Though it didn't seem to penetrate his brain at first how vital my mission was, presently he understood and entirely agreed with me that Athens should know.

As we rattled swiftly toward the city I pictured its tense and ominous quiet—and the cripple boy on the Acropolis lookout. Now as we entered the suburb, perhaps he had seen us and was shouting, "A taxi-cab! A taxi-cab!" There was so much dust I couldn't see the crowds of people that were no doubt following me to hear my message. The chauffeur and I spent half an hour looking for the market-place, where I was to tell 'em and fall dead, but much to my disgust I finally learned there *wasn't* any. Oh, well, I could tell Roderic, anyway. The taxi drove up to our hotel. Roderic was there in the dining-room holding forth as host for my birthday party. Exuberantly I rushed up to our guests and cried out that chivlizhayshun was shaved.

How meager indeed in these degenerate days are the rewards of heroism! In return for my self-sacrificing services to Athens, all I received was a look of mortified despair from my comrade, and a subsequent note from the hotel manager to the effect that if I were going to continue residing in his eminently respectable hostelry, would I *please* not be such a nut.

# ON THE TRAIL OF ULYSSES

# CHAPTER VII

## ON THE TRAIL OF ULYSSES

THE mountains of the mainland of Greece rose behind us; the mountains of an isle of Greece before, and all about us the blue Ægean sparkled in the brilliant summer sun. Roderic and I looked out upon this panorama of land and sea from beneath the awnings of a small, leisurely-moving steamer that we had boarded at Piræus shortly after my heroic return from Marathon. Having crept northward along the coasts of Attica and Eubœa, the little ship had now turned straight to the east and bravely headed for the rocky isle of Skyros right in the middle of the Ægean. From time to time we looked ahead inquisitively at the approaching island for we were soon to disembark upon its storied shores and make it our residence for a week.

A perfect picture of ennui, Roderic sprawled in his deck-chair trying to look bored, and succeeding very well. I sat beside him, busily engaged with my pen and note-book.

"Writing a love-letter to one of your Marble Maidens?" he asked with a tinge of ridicule.

"I'm writing books," I replied loftily. "I've just begun chapter seven. Want to hear it?"

"No-o-o!"

So I began to read:

" 'The year 1194 B. C. found ominous war clouds gathering over Greece. Paris, a Trojan Prince, had violated the home of Menelaus, King of Sparta, and carried off his beautiful wife, Helen, to Troy. It has been cynically intimated that Helen may have put Paris up to it. But Sparta didn't appreciate these circumstances, and with righteous indignation rushed to arms to bring back by force the errant lady. Bound by sacred treaty, Sparta's allies under the supreme command of Agamemnon, Menelaus' brother, came to her assistance, and at Aulis, forty miles north of Marathon, the hosts began to gather.' "

"That certainly is an original story," Roderic re marked sarcastically.

"Don't criticize so soon. That's only the historic background. Before I get too deep in this book I think I should explain to my readers—the oracle promised me a hundred thousand, you know—how Ulysses came to leave home, and where he went first on his travels—since we are going everywhere he went."

"I think so too. And how well you explain it! You don't even mention him."

"Oh, give me a chance. In the next paragraph I add that he was one of these allies. Listen to this:

" 'In his remote little island kingdom of Ithaca, Ulysses was loath to take part in a conflict so utterly unrelated to his own affairs. He had been married to Penelope, the most faithful of wives, not so long before, and a baby son, Telemachus, had made him the happiest and most contented king of all the Greek states. The very last thing on earth he wanted just now was to leave his happy home and go roystering off with an army to slaughter the citizens of an almost unknown city just because one of its princes had stolen somebody's wife who was probably no good anyway.

" 'The moment Ulysses realized, however, that it was impossible to escape his oath of allegiance he assembled his company of twelve hundred Ithacans, and his fleet of twelve ships. Having rounded Cape Malea,'—that's the southernmost tip of the Greek peninsula, Rod,—'he delivered his military contingent to Agamemnon at Aulis. There he threw his amazing vitality and enthusiasm into the Greek cause, and, with his crafty counsel, became the brains of the Greek army.'

"That brings him round to this side of Greece," I added, laying down my note-book, "and into our present territory. Aulis is just behind us on the other side of Euboea."

"If we're following Ulysses' trail, why didn't we start out from Ithaca, and come to Aulis?"

"Because we're going to Ithaca in the end,—if we aren't seduced by the lotus fruit, and you don't make a fool of yourself over some Siren. We didn't go to Aulis because there's no way to get from Aulis to Skyros."

"I don't understand *yet* why it's so necessary for us to take all this time out from our trip to Troy for a visit to Skyros,—that is, so far as our Odyssey is concerned. You did say something about Achilles being in hiding there, and about Ulysses going after him to bring him back to fight with the Greek army. I asked you if Achilles was a conscientious objector, and you gave a sigh of despair and bought me some chewing gum. That was probably just because you don't know yourself what it was all about."

"Then listen to this—and learn," I said, picking up my note-book again and turning to another page of chapter seven.

" 'In the Ægean, some seventy miles northeast of Athens, lies a rocky little island called Skyros. Though sadly neglected by nature it has its claims to immortality no less than the other long-celebrated isles of Greece. Delos is famed because it gave birth to Apollo and Diana; Cythera, because Venus was born from its waters: Lesbos. because in her palace there 'burning Sappho loved and sung.' The renown of these islands rests solely on their ancient glory, but Skyros can boast not only of an abundance of classic associations, but of possessing a modern halo as well. Its ancient fame is due to the fact that Achilles, the most heroic of the Homeric Greeks, made it the home of his late boyhood, and that it took no less a person than Ulysses to win him away. Skyros' modern distinction comes from its having sheltered, since April, 1915, the grave of one of the finest and brightest spirits that the twentieth century has produced.' I'm not going to mention *him* though till I get to the next chapter.

" 'Achilles,' " I continued reading, " 'at the time of his residence in Skyros was a comparatively unknown youth. He had been sent to the king's court there in the disguise of a girl, by Thetis, his mother, who, warned by the oracle of fatal consequences if he went with the Greeks to Troy, hoped to protect her son by thus removing him from the scene of danger. King Lycomedes, never dreaming that the tall handsome "maid" was not a girl, established him as lady-in-waiting upon Deidamia, his daughter.

" 'We do not know how soon Achilles revealed himself to Deidamia, but it was inevitable that they should fall in love,—his disguise notwithstanding. The princess and her "lady" became inseparable, and no one objected; they occupied the same apartment. and no one suspected.' "

Roderic would have interrupted me here with some facetious comment about such goings-on, had I not rushed ahead into the next paragraph.

" 'Meanwhile the Greek armies had gathered at Aulis and were ready to set sail, when a soothsayer confided to Agamemnon the fact that Troy would never fall without the aid of a young man by the name of Achilles. Wishing to leave nothing undone that might help the expedition to succeed, the Greek commander asked Ulysses to seek out this Achilles person and bring him to their ranks.

" 'By some unknown divination, Ulysses learned that the object of his quest was in hiding at the king's court at Skyros, and set out to find him.

" 'Disguised as a pedler, he gained access to Lycomedes' palace, and spread before all the court maidens an assortment of female finery, in the midst of which he had craftily placed a glittering shield, and a sword of bronze. Achilles instinctively pounced upon these beautiful weapons, and thus betrayed himself to the artful Ulysses. Once detected there was no great difficulty in persuading him to join his countrymen in the great war. Together the two young men that were destined to become the most celebrated characters in Homeric literature, left Skyros for Aulis. As for Achilles, the fateful prophecy of the oracle in due time came to pass.' "

"Did Deidamia shoot herself when her lover skipped off?" Rod asked with his usual irreverence.

But I never got to answer his question, for at this point a blast from the ship's whistle announced that we were drawing near the mountain-bound little harbor and must prepare to disembark.

Aboard the tender which came to meet us was a very agreeable young Greek. On hearing Rod and me speaking American he introduced himself to us in our own language. He knew the States well, having run a fruit store in Omaha. And when he learned that this city likewise claimed Roderic for its own, he looked upon my companion as a blood-brother, urging this fellow Nebraskan to accept his hospitality—such as it was,—during our visit.

While I did not hail from Omaha, and was therefore not of the sacred fraternity, he agreed that I might come along too.

What was his name?

"Achilles."

We fully expected him to add that his wife's name was Deidamia, and that she was the daughter of Lycomedes, the mayor, but on inquiring we found he didn't have a wife.

He *did* have one of the most picturesque homes on the island, in the little city likewise called Skyros, built upon the site of King Lycomedes' capital. Gleamingly white, the snug house was stuck precariously upon the side of the citadel hill, and buried under grape-vines.

When the afternoon of our first day's residence

here had cooled, and the shadows were lengthening,
Roderic, our host and I strolled along the beach beneath the towering cliffs, where the original Achilles,
draped modestly in his hateful garb, had walked beside his Deidamia. Then as the same deep violet hue
that suffuses Athens at sunset began to spread over
land and sea, Achilles from Omaha guided us up a
steep winding path that climbed to the decaying
citadel crowning the hilltop,—the same hilltop in all
probability where the palace of King Lycomedes had
stood. It took small imagination to picture the crafty
Ulysses himself, bent low under his pack of pedler's
wares, climbing our very path.

The sun had gone down before we reached the top,
but what a soft calm glow it had left behind. The
classic Achilles, looking out upon this same purple
picture, must have stood where we stood, and with
his Deidamia close beside him watched the island-
flecked Ægean fade on just such gentle summer eve-
nings as this evening. Here Ulysses spread his baubles before the maidens of the court; here Achilles
seized the sword and went to his destiny; here
Deidamia clung tearfully to him, the last night of
their union; here the princess sat, when he had sailed
away, and, looking across the sea toward Troy, be-
sought the gods to protect her lover and bring him
soon and safely back to her empty arms.

As we rested in the hilltop-darkness, vigorous

native music began to drift up to us from the big café on the square below,—a wedding, we were told. There was a wild syncopation to it, a shrill barbaric lilt, that set one's blood to tingling. Achilles, having dined us, led the way down to the animated scene of action and turned us loose among the revelers.

They were dancing the *sirtos,* a national Greek dance, the origin of which is lost in the past. Deidamia may have danced it with Achilles; Ulysses with Penelope; Helen with Paris (probably better than with Menelaus); Roderic and I danced it with the buxom black-eyed maids of Skyros whose children unto the tenth generation will dance it at every wedding festival such as this.

Being the only strangers present we were given a hearty welcome. *Mastika,* such as we had propitiated the angry Zeus with on Olympus, was poured in a continual stream into our glasses. Not to drink the distasteful fluid would seriously have offended our bridegroom host; to drink it was to run the risk of becoming as uproarious as the other guests. We drank.

The music grew wilder, the long line of dancers more reckless. Roderic and I broke into the jiggling circle, joining hands with these modern bacchanals. We jiggled on the right foot, jiggled on the left foot, stepped and dipped and stepped and dipped; jiggled on the right foot, jiggled on the left foot, stepped and

dipped and stepped and dipped. There was intoxication in the piercing pipes—hour after hour—men
and women—boys and girls—not one ever left the
dancing ranks except to seize another drink of
*mastika*. The wooden floor resounded to the
rhythmical stamp of our feet; there were shouts and
hot laughter; the leader of the swaying line, holding
by his left hand the bride, who in turn led the others,
pranced and leaped and twirled and postured, until
his legs could endure no more. The moment he
dropped from line another took his place, eager to
excel his predecessor's prowess.

Toward morning Rod and I had learned the
leader's antics as well as any one,—and drunk as much
*mastika*. The musicians, inexhaustible, were playing
more violently than ever, and swaying on their
benches, half delirious from their own music. In a
new outburst of enthusiasm one tottering old gray-
beard with a wild yell plunged into the circle alone
and cut the most amazing capers.

Away went the last leash on Rod's inhibitions.
A most dignified youth generally, he now became
fired with a sweeping impulse to lead the line. Snatch-
ing off Achilles' flaming red "cholera sash" he wound
it about his own waist, and, encouraged by the cheers
of the multitude, showed Skyros how *really* to lead
the *sirtos*. He added a clog to the jiggle; he clicked
his heels in the air; he kicked the candles out of the

chandelier; he was superb. And all about, led on by
the clogging, abandoned Roderic, the line jiggled on
the right foot, jiggled on the left foot, stepped and
dipped and stepped and dipped till the sun came up,
and the music died, and the last drop of *mastika* had
been drunk.

O Ulysses, if some Greek boy married some
Greek girl the night you arrived at Skyros, what a
perfectly *swell* time you must have had!

## "SOME CORNER OF A FOREIGN FIELD"

# CHAPTER VIII

## "SOME CORNER OF A FOREIGN FIELD"

IN THE starlight the gravestone of Rupert Brooke glimmered, wraith-like. How lonely it was—how desolate—how far, far away!

I stood beside the grave alone. The silence of the night enfolded land and ocean in dim mystery. The stars crept close to illuminate the name carved across the marble tomb,—a tomb that was to me a sacred shrine and the goal of another long pilgrimage.

I was a junior schoolboy at Lawrenceville when I read of Brooke's death and burial at Skyros in April, 1915. But already I had come under the spell of his poetry and placed him among my heroes. I wonder what I would have thought if I could have looked forward then to the great moment when I was to attain the very shores of Skyros, and on a clear summer night stand before the white stone slab that marks his burial place.

Even at that time I had wanted to make a pilgrimage to his grave, and the desire had grown with the

115

years. At eighteen I met an Englishman who had actually known Rupert Brooke. To me it was like meeting one of the apostles. Before I left Princeton I was reading everything about him I could lay my hands on, and attempting—as how many others have?—to write as he wrote. In fact Brooke's poetry became my Bible, for in it I found all my own groping ideas and intense youthful moods expressed as I could never hope to express them for myself.

If I was lonely,

"I saw the pines . . .
Very beautiful, and still, and bending over
Their sharp black heads against a quiet sky.
And there was peace in them, and I
Was happy, and forgot to play the lover . . ."

If I was melancholy,

"Tenderly, day that I have loved, I close your eyes,
And smooth your quiet brow, and fold your thin
dead hands . . ."

was melancholy too.

If I was hurt,

"All suddenly the wind comes soft,
And spring is here again; . . .
The hawthorn hedge puts forth its buds,
And my heart puts forth its pain . . ."

kept me company.

If I was homesick,

"Just now the lilac is in bloom,
All before my little room;
And in my flower-beds, I think,
Smile the carnation and the pink;
And down the borders, well I know,
The poppy and the pansy blow . . ."

comforted me.

If I was bitter *Jealousy* fed me the vinegar I
desired; and when I felt the exultation of living seething within,

"Crown the hair, and come away!
Hear the calling of the moon,
And the whispering scents that stray
About the idle warm lagoon.
Hasten, hand in human hand,
Down the dark, the flowered way,
Along the whiteness of the sand,
And in the water's soft caress,
Wash the mind of foolishness . . ."

was the song I chose to sing.

Alexander, Richard Cœur de Lion and Lord
Byron, the previous objects of my hero worship, were
cast aside; Rupert Brooke alone held my interest.

He was in my mind even on the last visit to the
Acropolis and my Marble Maidens. From this high
rock I looked toward the bay and tried to picture the
little isle where, at twenty-eight, Rupert Brooke had
closed the eyes, and smoothed the quiet brow, and

folded the thin dead hands of the last day that he had
loved.

From the summit of Mount Parnassus, some
weeks before, I had *seen* Skyros, for it was up through
this very isle, straight to the eastward, that the sun
had burst out of the Ægean. From this Altar of
Poetry—Parnassus itself—to watch the new day, the
renewed life of the world, breaking so gloriously over
Rupert Brooke's tomb, gave me an assurance of his
immortality that was more dramatic and more vivid
than all the monuments and all the eulogies with
which posterity has honored him.

Understanding, then, my personal reverence for
Brooke, one can appreciate my excitement when, in
searching for the trail of Ulysses, I learned that it
was to Skyros he had gone in quest of Achilles.

Immediately this barren little island became one
of the chief destinations of my travels in Greece. I
must go there because Ulysses had gone there; I
must go there because Rupert Brooke was still there.

It was not an easy journey. To visit the grave of
Rupert Brooke one must endure as difficult a fifteen
miles of jagged terrain as it is possible to imagine.
From noon till darkness Achilles and Roderic and I
picked our way on horseback along the trail: now
beside the sea indented with marble grottoes, the
home of the sea nymphs, where the water was im-
measurably deep and incomparably emerald; now

over the olive-dotted watershed across more miles of
pale pink rocks where the dwarf holly made deep
green patterns against the coral mountains. Color,
color, in land and sea—a great rock-garden fragrant
with sage and thyme, splashed with poppy red,
canopied by the bluest sky on earth, gilded by eternal
summer, set in the beryl Ægean that breaks upon
these marble shores with a fringe of snowy foam.
This is Skyros—this is the island where Rupert
Brooke died on a French hospital ship that happened
to be accompanying his Gallipoli-bound transport and
had anchored in a bay just off the southern coast.

The sun had gone down behind the mountain we
had crossed as we approached this bay. Our trail led
along the white sand of the twilight beach. Achilles
suddenly turned inland, following the dry bed of the
creek, and for a mile led us struggling up through
the undergrowth that blocked our way. Then, suddenly, a flat little plateau shaded by a circle of hoary
olive trees; and there in the center of these gray
mourners was the grave.

In his most poetic fancy Brooke could have desired no lovelier spot. On three sides the marble
mountains shield it; seaward there is a glorious vista
of the island-dotted ocean, bluer than the sky itself
which looks straight down through the wreath of olive
trees upon the tomb. The flowering sage that per-
fumes all of Skyros grows thickest here. There is a

sweetness in the air, a calmness in the ancient trees,
a song in the breeze through the branches, a poem in
the picture of the sea.

It is probable that Brooke discovered this enchanted spot himself. We know that with several
fellow officers from the Steamship *Grantully Castle*
he went ashore for a holiday, and having detected the
little plateau from the ship's deck, set out to explore
it. Is it not probable that one with his fine apprecia-
tions would have found the olive grove so appealing—
for it was at the height of a Grecian spring—that he
would have expressed his admiration for the spot to
his companions? And is it not likely that just three
days after, April 23, 1915, when he died with tragic
suddenness from blood poisoning, his companions
remembered and brought him back to rest forever
amid the trees where he had spent his last happy hour?

In Mr. Edward Marsh's memoir of Brooke there
is a letter which Mr. Denis Browne, one of his comrades at the time of his death, wrote to Marsh:

"We buried him . . . in an olive grove where
he had sat with us on Tuesday (three days before)—
one of the loveliest places on this earth, with gray
green olives round him, one weeping over his head;
the ground covered with flowering sage, bluish-gray,
and smelling more delicious than any flower I know.
The path up to it from the sea is narrow and difficult
and very stony. . . . We had to post men with
lamps every twenty yards to guide the bearers. . . .

Think of it all under a clouded moon—and those divine scents everywhere. We lined the grave with all the flowers we could find, and Colonel Quilter set a wreath of olive on the coffin. The funeral service was very simple, said by the Chaplain, and after the Last Post the little lamp-lit procession went once again down the narrow path to the sea."

Three days later Winston Churchill wrote to the London *Times*:

"Rupert Brooke is dead. A telegram from the Admiral at Lemnos tells us that his life has closed at the moment when it seemed to have reached its spring-time. A voice had become audible, a note had been struck, more true, more thrilling, more able to do justice to the nobility of our youth in arms engaged in this present war, than any other—more able to express their thoughts of self-surrender, and with a power to carry comfort to those who watched them so intently from afar. The voice has been swiftly stilled. Only the echoes and the memory remain; but they will linger.

"During the last few months of his life, months in preparation in gallant comradeship and open air, the poet-soldier told with all the simple force of genius the sorrow of youth about to die, and the sure triumphant consolations of a sincere and gallant spirit. He expected to die; he was willing to die for the dear England whose beauty and majesty he knew; and he advanced toward the brink in perfect serenity, with absolute conviction of the rightness of his country's cause, and a heart devoid of hate for fellow-men.

"The thoughts to which he gave expression in the very few incomparable war sonnets which he has

left behind will be shared by many thousands of
young men moving resolutely and blithely forward
into this, the hardest, the cruelest, and the least re-
warded of all the wars that men have fought. They
are a whole history and revelation of Rupert Brooke
himself. Joyous, fearless, versatile, deeply instructed, with classic symmetry of mind and body, he
was all that one would wish England's noblest sons
to be in days when no sacrifice but the most precious
is acceptable, and the most precious is that which is
most freely proffered."

Was it this premonition of inevitable death that
inspired Brooke to write, not long before his burial
in this far-away little island, his immortal sonnet?

"If I should die, think only this of me:
That there's some corner of a foreign field
That is forever England. There shall be
In that rich earth a richer dust concealed;
A dust whom England bore, shaped, made aware,
Gave, once, her flowers to love, her ways to roam,
A body of England's, breathing English air,
Washed by the rivers, blest by suns of home."

Twilight had gone, and the stars were gleaming.
Achilles had hobbled the horses and strolled off with
his blanket to find a less rocky bed. Roderic sought
a higher ledge where the tree-tops, below him, would
not interfere with his prospect of the sea and his
proximity to the sky. I was left alone. . . .

I stood beside the grave and thought how safe
Brooke was here. He had a beautiful burial place·

he had the brightest sky and the best sunsets in the world; and the whispering olive grove, and the view of the sea. He had once written:

". . . Safe shall be my going,
Secretely armed against all death's endeavor;
Safe though all safety's lost; safe where men fall;
And if these poor limbs die, safest of all."

"Safest of all"—for more than a decade now. And yet, though I looked down upon his very tomb and though I fully knew it was he who slept beneath it, the actuality of his death only vaguely impressed me. I had long ago drawn my own mental portrait of Brooke, and it had been so clear and so real, that whenever I thought of him, it was a living, breathing man my imagination pictured,—a living man who, as he once exclaimed about himself, "felt a burning hunger to do and do and do things, to walk a thousand miles, and write a thousand plays, and sing a thousand poems, and drink a thousand pots of beer, and kiss a thousand girls." Such self-revelations had shaped my picture; and with that picture this evidence of his death before me seemed utterly incompatible and incredible.

And just as he had never been a dead poet to me, so had he never been a stranger. True, I had never seen him in my life,—but that didn't matter. Had I not met him—in his poetry? And had I not shared

with him there his inmost thoughts, just as any one
else may do who reads it sympathetically? No one
ever wore one's heart on one's sleeve less than Rupert
Brooke, but he wore it bravely in his poetry. His
poetry is himself. It is charged with his own personality, his own exultations, and his own defeats. It
is intensely subjective. I had scarcely a friend about
whose mind and heart I knew as much as I felt I
knew about Rupert Brooke's, and I had learned it all
from the small volume of his poems which I had that
moment in my pocket.

How cool and clear the night had grown. The
moon behind the mountains must be rising. In this
new illumination my fancy began to speculate as to
what the future might have held for Brooke; as to
what he would have done after the war, had he been
spared by it. He died before he had half-fulfilled his
hopes. What were they . . .? His friends assure
us that whatever he did he would have clung to poetry.
He once said that for him there were only three good
things in the world: one was to read poetry, one was
to write poetry, and one was to live poetry. Had he
lived poetry it would have mattered very little what
else he did.

It was because of this dominant poetic strain in
his nature that he was so elated when he learned, on
sailing from England, that his transport was going
to Greece. He had not imagined fate could be so be-

nign. On entering the Ægean the realization suddenly came to him that the ambition of his life had
been to go on a military expedition against Constantinople; and that when he *thought* he was hungry,
or sleepy, or aching to write a poem,—*this* was what
he had really, blindly, wanted. Visions of fighting
the Turks on the plains of Troy filled his head. He
pictured Hero's tower crumbling under their fifteen-
inch guns. He was eager to see if the ocean was
"wine dark" and "unvintageable" as it always was in
Homer. He even began a poem on shipboard:

> "And Priam and his fifty sons
> Wake all amazed, and hear the guns,
> And shake for Troy again."

I found myself thinking of the interest a man
with Brooke's classical enthusiasms would have taken
in my Odyssey expedition. How he would have loved
to find the Lotus Land, and the Cyclops, and Scylla
and Charybdis, and the Sirens! What a romantic
thrill it would have given him to disembark on the
shores of Ithaca, and in his mind's eye follow the returned Ulysses to his palace door, and watch him
slaughter the hundred insolent suitors of Penelope!

The thought of Ithaca reminded me that my own
visit there would be the last chapter of this expedition.
From Ithaca I would turn westward again toward
America. Then the splendid idea came to me that I

might easily go to England on my way home, and
try to meet Brooke's mother and his friends at Rugby,
to report to them that his grave was still as beautiful
and peaceful as they would want it.   I realized I'd
rather meet Mrs. Brooke than the Queen of England.

And why not Cambridge also?  I could go there
from Rugby, and walk across the meadows to Grant-
chester, and call upon the Old Vicarage where Brooke
spent the happiest days of his life.   From its case-
ments I too might

> ". . . see the branches stir
> Across the moon at Grantchester!
> And smell the thrilling-sweet and rotten
> Unforgetable, unforgotten
> River-smell, and hear the breeze
> Sobbing in the little trees."*

So intent had I been on this beautiful new plan,
I had not noticed how the mountain ridge above had
begun to glow.   The darkness had faded perceptibly,
and the rocks and silver trees about me had become
clearly visible.   A shadow moved suddenly with the
wind beneath the olive grove.   A little startled I
watched it, half expecting Rupert Brooke's specter
to emerge.   Scrutiny proved it to be only a drooping
olive branch.   But the thought of seeing him abroad
on such a night as this brought to my mind the lines

*All this came to pass—months later.

from a poem in which a fellow-poet has expressed the
same thought:

"Once in my garret—you being far away
Tramping the hills and breathing upland air,
Or so I fancied—brooding in my chair,
I watched the London sunshine, feeble and grey,
Dapple my desk, too tired to labor more,
When looking up, I saw you standing there,
Like sudden April at my open door.

"Though now beyond earth's farthest hills you face,
Song-crowned, immortal, sometimes it seems to me
That, if I listen quietly,
Perhaps I'll hear a light foot on the stair,
And see you, standing with your angel air,
Fresh from the uplands of eternity."

Slowly from behind the mountaintop the last late
remnant of a dying moon crept up into the sky,
blanching the pale olive grove, and falling tenderly
upon the marble grave. . . .

". . . some corner of a foreign field
That is forever England . . .
. . . a richer dust concealed—
A dust whom England bore. . . ."

And I turned away to climb the rocks and find
Roderic, and lie wrapped in my blanket waiting for
the dawn.

# I SWIM THE HELLESPONT

# CHAPTER IX

## I SWIM THE HELLESPONT

WE ALL have our dreams. Otherwise what a dark and stagnant world this would be. Most of us dream of getting rich; many of us of getting married; and some of us of getting unmarried. I've met people whose great dream it was to visit Jerusalem, or Carcassonne, or to look upon the seven hills of Rome. I'll confess to a sentimental life-long dream of my own,—not of riches, or weddings, or Jerusalem, however,—something far less reasonable than that. I've dreamed of swimming the most dramatic river in the world—the Hellespont. Lord Byron once wrote that he would rather have swum the Hellespont than written all his poetry. So would I!

Sometimes, once in a long, long while, sentimental dreams come true. Mine did, and it was as colorful and satisfying as all my flights of fancy had imagined it would be. To me the Hellespont was not just a narrow strait of cold blue water, discharging the Black Sea and the Sea of Marmora into the Ægean. Far more than that: it was a tremendous symbol,—a symbol of audacity, of challenge; of epic poetry, and heroic adventure.

The nature of the Hellespont's first records seem to have set an example for all the historic events that have clustered about it. Its very naming is a dramatic story. The name of "Hellespont" ("Dardanelles" on the modern maps) goes back to legendary ages, receiving its title from "Helle," the King of Thessaly's daughter who fell into the channel from the winged ram with the golden fleece, on whose back she was fleeing from her enemies.

Through this same Hellespont, Jason, in his immortal ship, the *Argo,* sailed in quest of this same fleece. For ten years, from 1194 to 1184 B. C., the fleets of the Greeks were beached at its entrance, while their armies, led by Agamemnon, Achilles and Ulysses, thundered at the lofty walls of Troy. It was across this stream that Leander nightly swam to keep his clandestine trysts with Hero. In the very wake of Leander, in one of the most spectacular military exploits in history, King Xerxes of Persia, the mightiest ruler of his time, crossed from Asia to Europe with a colossal army for the invasion of Greece. Here in the following century Alexander the Great ferried his Macedonians from Europe to Asia to begin his conquest of the world. Back once more in the fourteenth century rolled the tide of invasion from east to west: this time the Turkish con-

Lord Byron's house at Abydos occupied by the poet at the time of his Hellespont swim in 1818.

The Abydos Peninsula—the goal of my swim—seen from Xerxe's Mound. The Hellespont current is deflected by this obstruction toward the European shore opposite.

Entering the Hellespont for the five-mile swim to Abydos.

Looking toward Abydos Point from the Sestos acropolis at the foot of which is the traditional site of Hero's tower.

quests that were to turn the Hellespont from that
day to this into Saracenic property. Through this
strait the piratical Turkish cruisers moved for generations, making all the eastern Mediterranean a Turkish lake. Since 1600 Russia has fought periodic wars
for the possession of this storied channel. And now
the shores of this same Hellespont are dotted with
the wrecks of sunken Allied battle fleets and strewn
with the graves of a hundred thousand French and
English soldiers, whose blood was squandered in
rivers in the desperate attempt in 1915 to plant the
Allied flags over the rocks where Hero joined her
drowned romantic lover in dim antiquity. Indeed
one's spirits surge to read the amazing record of this
fateful stream and realize how repeatedly it has
shaped the destiny of the world.

This, then, is the Hellespont, and the scene where
my dream came true.

Nature was most capricious when she created
this eccentric corner of the earth. She drives the
enormous volume of the Black Sea past Constantinople through a narrow channel called the Bosporus—
and then again by more reluctant, prolonged, tortuous
degrees, through a winding canal-like gash in the
mountains, forty miles long, and from one to five
miles broad. Down this insufficient Hellespont, with
Europe on her right side and Asia on her left, the
Black Sea, unleashed at last, rushes at top speed,

foaming with indignation at her long imprisonment. For ten thousand years she has poured herself into the greater ocean, season in and season out. Tides she scorns. South—south—south, her waters always swirl so that one may well call the strait a river since but for its briny nature it qualifies in every respect to this term.

Few water-courses can boast of having seen the rise and fall of as many stately cities on its banks as can the Hellespont. Of these the two most familiar to us (though they have long since crumbled into dust) are Sestos and Abydos: the former on the European side of the narrowest part of the Hellespont; the latter almost opposite on the Asian, some three miles away. And why are these two cities, from among the scores of their contemporaries, alone favored with immortality? Is it because of their great military conquests, or their celebrated soldiers, or their marble temples? No, none of these. They are immortal because a youth—an undistinguished, unde-scribed youth of Abydos, named Leander—tragically loved an equally undistinguished maid of Sestos named Hero: and legends of love refuse to die.

One loved fiercely in legendary Greece. Hero, priestess of a temple though she was and consequently sentenced to a loveless life, was no less human than her lay-sisters. She craved love as they, and when, on the occasion of the popular Sestos Temple festival,

her eyes caught the concentrated glance of a graceful
and sturdy youth, she did not run away. The moment
he guardedly spoke to Hero, her vows, her veil, quite
properly, lost their power. She learned that his name
was Leander and that he had sailed across the straits
in his boat from his home in Abydos to attend the
festival. They must not be seen together, since she
was a priestess, prohibited by the gods from the
society of man—*by day*. But that night, might he
come in the moonlight, to the temple garden? Find
me the girl of ancient Greece, or modern Greece, or
any other land, who would have said no.

And so they met in secret, high on the Sestos cliffs,
and looked out over the glittering ripples of the
Hellespont that swirled ceaselessly past. And the
next night again, and the next. All went well until
one of the temple orderlies saw the lovers together and
betrayed them to his superiors.

In a rage the head priest seized the unfortunate
girl. He dragged her down the cliff-path to the very
edge of the Hellespont, and then up to the top of a
tower where the wretched maiden was left in solitary
imprisonment, safe from the approach of any more
sacrilegious lovers.

From his homeward-bound boat Leander, in the
moonlight, had witnessed the figures entering the
tower-prison that rose above the wave-lapped rocks,
and in his heart he rejoiced. They were casting her

into his very arms—for he was the strongest swimmer in Abydos.

Impatiently from his Asiatic shore he watched the sun go down beyond the cliffs of Sestos, across the swirling Hellespont.  While they were only three miles away, it was necessary to take horse and servant and ride up-stream along the Abydos side until he reached a point well above Sestos.  Sestos lay sharply up-stream, and the tideless current, squeezing through the narrowing channel, raced past at such a rate that no swimmer, save a god, could have swum against it.  From above, though it would require four miles or more of furious swimming to reach Hero's tower and not be carried past, he might hope to suc‐ceed.

Strange and desperate things are done in the name of love.  Shortly after nightfall, Leander, ready to face any obstacle for one caress of his mistress, plunged into the Hellespont.  He had hoped Hero would guide him by means of a light from her tower window—nor was he disappointed.  A spark from her small oil lamp cast a faint path across the water.  Thus directed he steered his course to Sestos, and drew himself up on the rocks beneath the tower.  Hero was half expecting him to come, and watching.  Tearing the cover of her couch into strips she made a rope by which on the hidden off-shore side he could pull himself up to her apartment.  And then, what an eager reunion!

*Partir, c'est toujours mourir un peu.* Yet part they must, while darkness hid them.

The journey back, though difficult and cold and unrewarded, was not so long as the first crossing, for the Abydos point extended deep into the stream and assisted the swimmer to reach the Asian shore.

Did I not say that love drives us to desperate ends? Again the next night, undiscouraged, unsubdued by the sinister river's power, Leander swam his way back to Hero's arms,—and many nights that followed.

But high on Olympus the fates were spinning to an end the immortal lovers' thread of destiny. They saw the storms and the winds that were churning the Hellespont as winter seized the land; they saw the madness for Hero that burned increasingly in Leander's heart, driving him recklessly into the face of any danger. Indeed, whom the gods would destroy, they first make mad.

And it *was* madness for the youth to defy the furies on such a night as this, and attempt as usual to swim across to his mistress' tower. Heaven and earth warned him back. But Hero's eyes beckoned, and to them he surrendered. Plunging through the surf he met the oncoming rollers. He looked anxiously for the little lighthouse. Nowhere was it to be seen, for the storm had obliterated the faithful lamp.

The usual hour of Leander's arrival had come and long since gone; and dawn, shrill and ominous and glowering, found Hero still at her heart-breaking vigil. And then she saw that Leander had come at last. There on the seething rocks below her window, the strong white body of her lover lay, tossed at her feet by some pitying water god. A flame swept through Hero's heart. In despair she cried out Leander's name, and plunged from her window into the swirling waters.

And so to-day because a man died for a maid, and a maid for a man, Sestos and Abydos are not forgotten as were their great contemporaries. Time annihilates all things but romance. In every land, in every generation it is romance that the human heart perpetuates. I do not doubt that in some distant time, when our modern world is dust, the story of Hero and Leander will stir mankind far more than all the futile foolishness of our own unheroic age.

Three thousand years later, Lord Byron was so gripped by the sapphire beauty of the Hellespont, and by the drama of its storied shores, that he ceased his restless wanderings and for an entire year rested in a charming little house at the very edge of the water near the site of Abydos. Like every true romanticist, Byron was deeply moved by the story of Leander, and decided, being a swimming enthusiast, to try to swim the Hellespont himself.

Early in April, 1818, accompanied by a friend, he undertook the crossing from Sestos to Abydos. Finding the water of an icy chilliness, the two swimmers postponed their venture until the following month. It was the third of May when the attempt was made again, and although, as Byron wrote in one of his note-books, "the water was still extremely cold from the melting of the mountain snows, we swam from Sestos to Abydos." This was slightly incorrect, because, as the poet added, he began the swim high above Sestos to make sure of gaining the sand point at Abydos. "The whole distance," he continues, 'from the place where we started to our landing on th. other side including the length we were carried by the current was computed roughly by our companions at upward of four English miles, though the actual breadth is less than two. The rapidity of the current is such that no boat can row directly across. Its rate of flow may be estimated by the fact that the whole distance was accomplished in one hour and ten minutes. The English consul at Dardanelles could not remember the straits ever having been swum before, and tried to dissuade me from the attempt. The only thing that surprised me was that, as doubt had been entertained of the truth of Leander's story, no traveler had heretofore endeavored to ascertain its practicality."

The poet, on landing safely at Abydos, in one of

his typically facetious moods, celebrated his swim in the following familiar verses:

"If in the month of dark December,
  Leander, who was nightly wont
(What maid will not the tale remember?)
  To cross thy stream, broad Hellespont!

"If, when the wintry tempest roar'd
  He sped to Hero, nothing loth,
And thus of old thy current pour'd,
  Fair Venus! How I pity both!

"For *me*, degenerate modern wretch,
  Though in the genial month of May,
My dripping limbs I faintly stretch,
  And think I've done a feat to-day.

"But since he cross'd the rapid tide,
  According to the doubtful story,
To woo,—and—Lord knows what beside,
  And swam for Love, as I for Glory;

" 'Twere hard to say who fared the best:
  Sad mortals! Thus the gods still plague you;
He lost his labor, I my jest;
  For he was drowned and I've the ague."

It was not many years after this that Byron followed Leander to Hades. However, the house in which the poet lived at Abydos on the edge of the Hellespont continues to stand intact to the present day, for Roderic and I occupied it.

In the actual wake of Ulysses at last, we had left

Skyros behind, and, like Ulysses, returned to the mainland of Greece,—he (proudly escorting Achilles) to reunite with his fleet, we to find a ship that would take us to Troy at the entrance to the Hellespont.

We found such a ship, but not being on the war-path for the recovery of anybody's wife, as was Ulysses, and having all the time we wanted to indulge in side excursions, we did not disembark at once on the long sandy shore of the Trojan plain where the eleven hundred and eighty-six Greek ships were drawn for ten long years. Instead we passed by for the moment, a stone's throw from it, and twenty miles on up-stream to Abydos, to investigate the Hellespont swim.

We found any "investigation" unnecessary. The sites of Sestos and Abydos were conspicuously, un-mistakably, there. At the former place the acropolis ruins establish its exact location. The Mound of Xerxes, up the slopes of which Abydos climbed, and the sand peninsula, which is a spur of the mound, establish Abydos with equal certainty. The only way to "investigate" my ability to swim the intervening distance was to dive in and swim. As previous en-durance tests I had swum the Nile and the Mississippi, but either of these was mere paddling compared with the Hellespont.

The first problem was to reach Sestos, the start-

ing point, in a boat big enough to buck the savage
current, and yet small enough to escort and safeguard
me on my return journey.  The Turkish officials
(suspecting we were British spies) made this exas-
peratingly difficult.  In order to move at all against
the relentless flow of the water and constant south
wind it was necessary to push off at four A. M., at
which time the elements were comparatively calm.
Each morning for a week the police delayed our
departure till almost noon by which time all the oars
and sails we could muster were utterly futile to combat the onslaught of the current.

Each day with renewed determination we tried
to beat and tack our way up-stream with every device
in our power.  Back and forth, back and forth, sailing endless miles in the blistering sun, trying to gain
a yard.  Then by sunset, utterly exhausted, we would
look back toward the Asiatic shore to find we were
still just off the Byron house, *exactly* where we'd
been that noon.

On the eighth day, in desperation, we managed
to sail straight across to the European shore, and,
though we were almost as far from Sestos as ever, we
were at least free of the obnoxious and suspicious
Asiatic officials.

That night we spent in one of the Gallipoli battle-
field graveyards, with thousands of wooden markers
of thousands of British soldiers spreading grimly

across the hillsides. We slept on the ground, using a grave for a pillow. Next morning long before daybreak, when the wind was stilled, Roderic and the two boatmen and I each took an oar, and heading our sailboat straight up-stream, bent to the task. One moment's relaxation, and we would lose ground. For five hours we fought our way toward Sestos—and attained it. But this was not enough. Being by no means a swimmer of Leander's caliber I thought it wise to take the precaution Byron had taken, and continue on up-stream some two miles more above Sestos in order to give myself more time to get across before the current swept me past Abydos point.

Finding a semi-sheltered cove, we anchored our craft and waded ashore for a rest. From the top of the bluff we could see Abydos dimly visible through the summer haze—about five miles away. Up to this moment we had been much too busy to think about a meal. Now with our first object attained we turned ravenously to our provision basket. It was absolutely empty. During the night the two Turkish boatmen had consumed every vestige of our food. Not so much as a crumb of bread was left. No, not quite as bad as that,—a small can of Norwegian sardines they had been unable to open. It was this or nothing. Roderic, realizing I had to make the swim, magnanimously insisted I consume the entire available supply of fuel; so I did.

Then at two o'clock I removed my clothing, and, my heart pounding with excitement, stood at the water's edge, praying to the water gods to deliver me safely on the other side. The summer sunshine blazed from a cloudless sky upon the sinister, sapphire stream that lapped invitingly at my feet. With nerves keyed up to the highest pitch, I yet held back in fear lest I fail. Despite the fact that Xerxes had scourged the Hellespont with chains in punishment for having destroyed his bridge of boats, I knew its beautiful, villainous waters had not been humbled. Here was my Siren Dream, beckoning to me. This was the Great Hour. I recalled a similar moment, in Japan, when on a zero January morning I faced the iceberg of Fujiyama at the timber line, ready to plunge up the glassy slopes to the blizzard-swept summit. Again, and stronger, came the spiritual exultation, the sudden strange pulse of power that makes cold chills of courage race through one's blood. My body whispered: "You can not possibly swim five miles in such a current," but Inspiration shouted: "This is the *Hellespont*—what matter if it's fifty!"

I plunged.

The Asiatic shore across the channel rose hazily. I struck out straight for it, with Roderic and the boat hovering close beside.

Before I had gone half a mile, whatever "form" I may have begun with soon vanished, and I thought

only of covering the greatest possible distance with
the least possible exertion: back-stroke, side-stroke,
dog-paddle, idle floating, any old thing to keep going.
A big Greek steamer bore upon us, rushing furiously
down-stream. It was our place to get out of the way.
The officers on the bridge, not seeing me in the water,
made frantic gestures. To protect me our sailboat
stood its ground in the very path of the oncoming ship,
and the steamer had to take a violent veer to one side
to keep from colliding with our craft. As she passed
by, not forty feet away, the officers hurled upon our
heads every unprintable name in their broad vocab-
ulary,—but it was all Greek to us.

By half past two I looked back toward Europe
to find, to my alarm, that I was already abeam the
Sestos bluffs. It made me realize how relentlessly I
was being swept down-stream. And Xerxes' Throne,
the conspicuous last-chance goal above Abydos, where
the Persian king sat to watch his army cross the
Hellespont on a bridge of boats over the very channel
I was swimming, seemed to have moved laterally
miles up the coast, though not toward me.

Before three o'clock I was in mid-stream. The
wind had constantly increased, and was now churning
the water with white caps. Every few minutes I was
half drowned when the resentful waves broke unexpectedly over my head. It seemed to me I swallowed
half the Black Sea. Nausea seized me so painfully

that several times I was ready to give up. But the in‹ creasing cold was the worst thing of all. The water flows so rapidly, even the surface has no opportunity to be warmed by the sun. After the first hour I began to grow uncomfortably numb.

However, the Throne of Xerxes was not far off now. All along, this had been a guide-point. And yet, as I drew near to it, I realized the ricocheting current was sweeping me parallel to the shore about ten times as fast as I was approaching it. The trees and rocks began to gallop past. From mid-stream I had calculated that I would land half a mile above the tip of Abydos point, but the mile soon became a quarter, a sixth, a tenth. After two hours in the water, within three hundred feet of shore I was being swept past the "last chance" of solid ground, just as, and where, Leander had been swept twenty-five hundred years before . . . and should I fail to reach the beach by ever so little, the current would drag me across the Hellespont, back to the European shore whence I had started.

Never have I felt such utter despair: a five-mile swim—my Hellespont—to miss achievement by one hundred yards! Never have I struggled so des- perately. My eyes became blurred, seeing only the land not far from me. I ceased to know where I was, or what I was doing, here in this cold, tormenting, boundless ocean. Mechanically I thrashed the water with my weary arms and legs.

Then—bump!—my *knees* struck bottom. I was swimming hysterically in less than three feet of water, for the shore sloped so gradually that, even at three hundred feet out, the water was not waist deep. With not one second to lose, I stood upright, and staggered ashore, with Rod, who had jumped into the surf, right beside me, and flopped on the last foot of ground at the point.

And so the Hellespont, that treacherous and briny river, was swum once more. Though I am but one of several to have battled successfully with its evil current, I have a distinction no one else can claim. Leander swam to look into a lady's eyes; Lord Byron, that he might write another poem; but I can boast of being the only person, dead or alive, who ever swam the Hellespont on a can of sardines!

# CHAPTER X

## THE WINDY WALLS OF TROY

IF YOU had to choose the most romantic corner in the world, what corner would you choose? I know mine. It is a corner that has fired imagination for three thousand years. It is a corner packed with stirring drama, touched by pathos and deluged with poetry. Such bitter tragedy it has known; such vivid personalities. It is the corner that Homer has immortalized in the first great masterpiece of European literature. It is Troy.

How many a night, as a very small boy, I was rocked to sleep in my father's lap to the romantic tales of this romantic city. Hector and Paris, Ajax and Achilles and the crafty Ulysses were my intimate childhood companions. A hundred times and more I heard the story of the wooden horse, until, if my father failed to recite every smallest word in the telling, I would know it and solemnly correct him. And a hundred times my eyes filled with tears when we came to the place where, in the final sack of the city,

Achilles' son, Pyrrhus, slew the good King Priam
on his very altar, and where the little son of Hector
was torn from his mother's arms to be hurled from
the walls. Oh, how I loved Hector, and how I hated
the arrogant Achilles! No Trojan could have lamented more bitterly than I the sight of Achilles'
chariot dragging the body of my favorite up and
down beneath the walls, before the eyes of his wife
and mother and father. I never forgave Achilles this.
It only increased my pro-Trojan sympathies, and
made me suffer the more that my heroic unconquerable Troy should fall before the miserable treachery
of a wooden horse.

How vividly my five-year-old eyes saw it all from
the high battlements of my father's lap. How many
beastly Greeks (before I went to sleep) I pursued
in wild flight across the Trojan plain, back to their
ships at the edge of the Hellespont! I never grew
tired of Troy and its bloody drama. *These* stories
had guts. Peter Rabbit! Uncle Remus! Bah!
They were for idiot children.

The years passed, but not my ardor for Troy.
Many of my childhood friends became strangers, but
not Hector, nor King Priam, nor the ever interesting
Ulysses. I go to sleep once more with Greeks and
Trojans battling in my brain, not curled up on my
father's lap, but stretched beneath the stars on top the
walls of Troy itself, against which the Greeks flung

their armies for ten long years in the most celebrated
siege in history. For twice ten years I had sought to
attain these very walls. I had arrived at last.

And I had come the same way Ulysses had
come,—from the sea. The Hellespont business with
its struggle and its surrender, its exhaustion and its
exultation, lay several days away. I was still suffering from the cold, but I was inexpressibly happy.
From the end of the sand pit where I lay for a few
moments, none too conscious, Roderic had dragged
me back to the boat and, in a determined effort to revive benumbed circulation, beat me till I howled for
mercy. Lord Byron remarked in his Hellespont
poem that the Hellespont gods were a very plaguing
lot for they had given him the ague and drowned
Leander. I didn't know exactly what the "ague"
was before my own adventure with the Hellespont
gods. I certainly learned.

That night, back at the Byron House, I shivered
and shook and swallowed brandy in the very same
room and for the very same cause his Lordship had
shivered and shaken and swallowed brandy a hundred
years before. Between the shakes and shivers Rod
and I discussed transportation to Troy. Byron made
the forty-mile round-trip journey on horseback from
"our" house. The fatigue that resulted he offers as
one of the reasons why he failed in his first attempt
at the Hellespont swim. undertaken immediately fol-

lowing the ride. After we looked at the dilapidated horses, and the wooden saddles still in service, we didn't wonder. They only made us resolve more firmly to cover the twenty miles by water as any good disciple of Ulysses should.

So a second time (having just passed close by the first time), we drew near the curving strand on the Asiatic side of the entrance to the Hellespont, where in 1194 B. C. eleven hundred and eighty-six Greek ships had been beached on their arrival from Aulis. Here the Trojans, having hastened from the gates of their city three miles inland, were drawn up await- ing the first onset of the enemy.

The oracle had prophesied that victory should be the lot of that side from which the first victim of the war should fall. Knowing this, Protesilaus, a Greek, drove his ship forward in order that of the thousand vessels, it should be the foremost prow impressed upon the sand, and leaped to the beach into the midst of the shouting Trojans to perish instantly at the hand of none other than Hector himself.

Eight hundred years after, 334 B. C., Alexander the Great, in his conquest of Asia and the world, pushed his own ship ahead exactly as Protesilaus had done, so that he himself might be able to leap ashore where the Greek ships had been drawn, and be the first of all his army to tread on Asian soil.

There were no shouting Trojans to obstruct Roderic's and my disembarking, nor any Macedonian armies to applaud. Only a few curious sea-gulls screamed at us as we lowered the sail of our *caique* in preparing to land.

Our boat having departed, we made a reconnaissance of our position. The bluff of Rhœteum, topped by the tomb of Ajax, rose at our left; the promontory of Sigeum, topped by the tombs of Achilles and his friend Patroclus, at our right. These rocky landmarks have not changed a foot since the ships of the Greeks first sighted them. But the two miles of marsh-land, river delta and beach, between, may have receded or advanced several hundred yards during the three thousand years that have passed. It could not have been far from our point of disembarkation, however, that the Greeks established and occupied their fortified shore-camp.

Sighting the village of Kum-Kale a short distance down the beach, we struck out toward it, crossing en route the almost dry bed of the Scamander River where it empties into the sea. At the village we found a road which we were told led to "Hissarlik" (the modern Turkish term for the site of Troy). One mile, two miles, three miles, we followed this trail across the plain where the Trojans had pursued the Greeks, and the Greeks in turn the Trojans. How many a heroic warrior had fallen in our path! And the gods, even Zeus himself, had moved upon this honored ground to assist the army they favored. The midsummer sun beat down upon us; the stones in the road were sharp and painful. But none of these things did we heed. We noticed only the abrupt flat-topped hillock that now rose before us,—all that was left of the lofty walls of Troy.

It was a thrilling moment. The same picture had opened up before the eyes of King Xerxes four hundred and eighty years before Christ. In that year the great Persian, leading his vast army toward the Hellespont, "reached the Scamander River and went up to the citadel of Priam, desiring to see it." One hundred and forty-six years later, Alexander, having survived his dramatic leap into the brine, crossed the plain as Xerxes had done before him, and came upon the ruins of Troy. He was only twenty-two at the time of his visit and, being an incorrigible romanticist, was imbued with as much hero-worship as any other young man at this romantic time of life. He claimed descent from Achilles, his great example as a man and inspiration as a warrior. In imitation of this heroic ancestor's pursuit of Hector three times around the walls of Troy, the young Alexander, before entering the sacred city, removed his heavy armor and ran three times, in the tracks of Achilles, around the walls. Having honored his hero in this way, he carried a garland of flowers over to the shore of the Ægean and placed it reverently on the tomb of the great Achilles.

The Romans believed Troy to be the cradle of their race, for was not Æneas, who planted the first seed of their empire in Italy, a Trojan hero who had escaped death at the hands of the Greeks when the city fell? In consequence, a long series of Roman emperors came to the Troad and with beating hearts made a sacred pilgrimage across this same blood-stained ground. Julius Cæsar came here in 48 B. C. and thought seriously of making Troy the capital of the Roman Empire. Augustus, Hadrian, Marcus Aurelius and a dozen more great Romans landed on the Troad shores and came to Troy along the same route Rod and I were following in quest of the most romantic corner of the world.

The mound took shape as we drew near,—a serried, creviced mound some eighty-five feet high and a third of a mile in circumference. Eagerly we reached its base. There I suddenly stopped and began to take off my shirt.

"Dick!" my companion exclaimed. "Put your clothes on. You know how easily you sunburn."

"Just taking off my armor, Rod. Here, hold the shining greaves," I said, handing him my pants.

"*Now* what are you going to do?" He was always fearful of my foolish enthusiasms.

"I'm going to do an Alexander the Great, stoopid. Get out the alarm clock and see how long it takes me. And when I've passed by the third time, drop your

red bandana so I'll know. It would be so unclassical
if I got mixed up and ran around four times, wouldn't
it?"

"Shall I climb to the tower and pretend I'm
Helen?" he asked with a touch of sarcasm.

"Oh, yes," I agreed. "With your mustache you
look *just* like her."

The rocks he threw at me fell short, for I had departed on my "circumcursation."

There is a wagon road around three sides of the
mound. The fourth side is over a rough spur upon
the extremity of which Troy was built. Running was
easy enough along the road; only the hillock was difficult to cross, for there was no path, and I had to pick
my way among trenches and brambles.

Roderic refused to take my homage to Achilles
seriously. As I passed beneath his "tower" the first
time, he threw more rocks and ribaldries at me. I
ignored his irreverence and trotted on.

At the second turn he dropped his red bandana
from the mound top, but I wouldn't be fooled. I
*knew* he was just trying to deceive me. The third
circuit ended in a burst of glory and perspiration.
The entire run of a mile had taken scarcely ten
minutes. I hope, however, that neither Achilles nor
Alexander was as hot and thirsty when they finished
as I.

"Now I suppose you'll want to walk the three

miles back to Kum Kale and scatter daisies on
Achilles' tomb just because Alexander did," was the
greeting I got from Rod.

"What a noble idea!" I really thought so. "And
you can put a garland on Patroclus' tomb. Achilles
and Patroclus; Alexander and Hephæstion; Roderic
and Richard. Let me have my shining greaves, Rod.
We can be over there in less than an hour."

"I'll not stir one foot," he exclaimed. "The bats
in your belfry multiply like rabbits. You haven't
even *seen* Troy,—you've just run around it, and you
want to go dashing off to sentimentalize over somebody's tomb, who, I'll bet, isn't buried there anyway.
It's two o'clock and I'm going to have lunch if I have
to eat it off your prostrate form. You never *would*
take time to eat or sleep if it weren't for me."

"Oh, all right." When Rod did get stubborn he
was a regular tyrant. "Let's have a look at the
beans."

After lunch we climbed together to the highest
point of the mound to look about. A tossing sea of
trenches and broken walls and ruins spread before
us, without order or significance,—the abandoned excavations of Schliemann and Dörpfeld, the two
celebrated German archeologists who first uncovered
Troy a generation ago. Few of the trenches penetrate the outer slopes, so that from the plain the
mound appears almost as undisturbed as the day

these "scientists of the spade" first saw it.  Only when
the rim has been gained, and the "crater" spreads before one does the vastness and completeness of the
excavation become evident.

Few achievements in archeological records have
been as full of interest as the unearthing and redis-
covery of Troy.  Until 1870 "Hissarlik," covered
with grass and underbrush, was to all appearances
just another flat-topped hillock rising out of the
broad, rather barren plain that encloses it on three
sides.  But in 1870, Doctor Heinrich Schliemann, a
man of consuming enthusiasms, assaulted the mound
with the firm belief that it was the site of Troy and if
explored would reveal more than rock and earth.

His hope was amply realized, for by digging to the
bottom of the hill he uncovered the remains of *nine*
successive cities built one on top of the other, the
bottommost dating from 3000 B. C.; the topmost
being of elaborate Roman construction and lost to
view about 500 A. D.  Doctor Schliemann naturally
believed the Homeric Troy was one of the lowest lay-
ers of ruins, not realizing that five prehistoric settle-
ments had preceded it.  It was only after his death
in 1890 that his successor, Doctor Wilhelm Dörpfeld,
discovered that the sixth layer from the bottom and
third from the top was the long lost Troy.  It had
escaped previous detection because the Roman build-
ers in leveling the Homeric ruin for their own citadel

nad scraped off the higher masonry in the center and
dumped it on top the lower at the edges. Schliemann
digging in the middle of the hill thus missed the object
of his quest. It was only when Dörpfeld encountered
the outer rim that the true situation came to light.
That Schliemann after twenty years of unfailing
faith and unwearying toil should have died just before the great discovery, was a tragedy indeed.

It has been more than fifty years since the excavations were first begun, and some thirty since they
were abandoned. In consequence, grass and debris
have once more begun to claim their own. Even
so, since several of the trenches are fifty feet deep and
a number of the uncovered walls thirty feet high, it
will take another lapse of centuries before the ruins
of the nine Troys are once more buried from view.

Of the sixth city very little remains, for even before Homeric Troy was razed by the Romans, local
conquerors had made a stone quarry of its walls to
fortify new cities in the surrounding country. In fact
only one Homeric wall of imposing dimension stands,
and one great tower facing the Hellespont. But this
tower fortunately is part of the Scæan Gate which
played such a heavy rôle in the *Iliad*. All the other
conspicuous ruins are Roman.

Eagerly, Roderic and I, on distinguishing this
landmark made our way to the top of the Scæan
Tower. The wind, sweeping always southward down

the Hellespont, blew steadily against us. "Windy Troy!" How often Homer mentions the wind! I well understand why this tower was the chief observation post of the city. All about us spread the treeless, uninhabited Trojan plain with the sparkling blue Hellespont clearly visible three miles away. The islands of Imbros and Tenedos loomed out of the ocean to the west, and far to the south, half lost in summer haze, Mount Ida, the station from which Zeus watched the great conflict, dominated the scene. The Scamander and Simois Rivers, so frequently mentioned by Homer, still drain the Trojan plain, but in summer they are only dry beds and so were invisible from our tower. Farther along on the narrow spur, the end of which is crowned by the ruins, one sees a Turkish farming village built of mud and purloined blocks of hallowed Trojan marble. From this village an occasional farm-hand comes to greet strangers and ask for *baksheesh.* Otherwise not a human being is to be seen.

Enthroned upon the very stones where Helen had pointed out to Priam all the Greek leaders assembled in the plain, and for ten years had watched her Greek kinsmen and her adopted Trojans slaughter one another in her name, I sat all afternoon with Homer's wind burning my face and whipping the grubby pages of my schoolboy *Iliad* carefully brought from America in anticipation of this magic moment. There

I vividly relived the drama that I had first taken part in upon my father's lap.

With my imagination aroused by the history all about me, I read and read and read, at fever heat. The *Iliad* ceased to be words on paper. It lived and it throbbed. I tried to shake off all modernity, and be a Trojan.

The thrilling pages turn and turn. Paris bearing the easily persuaded, immortally beautiful Helen, lands on the Hellespont shore and brings her into the city through the Scæan Gate. From my tower the Trojans descry the thousand ships of the pursuing Greeks, creeping over the horizon far out in the Ægean, and marshal on the shore to oppose them. Protesilaus perishes, but the Trojans retire to the city. For nine years they are besieged. Then when Troy is wearying of the struggle, Achilles, the bulwark of the Greeks, withdraws from the fight because of his quarrel with Agamemnon, and Hector, taking the offensive, kills Patroclus, Achilles' greatest friend.

Maddened with grief and rage over the loss of one so dear to him, Achilles with a grim thirst for revenge reenters the ranks and after a furious quest for Hector meets him below my Scæan Tower. Before the murderous eyes of the flashing Greek even the bravest of the Trojans quails. He turns to escape. Once, twice, thrice, around the walls of Troy, the doomed Hector flies. Hecuba and Priam, his royal parents, and Paris and Helen watch with anguished eyes from this tower-top.

On the opposite side of the city Hector tries to gain the Dardanian Gate. Achilles interposes. There is a desperate fight to the death which we can not see. I pray to Zeus, as I prayed at five years old, to give Hector courage, to go to his aid, not to let him perish miserably at the hand of Achilles. But the pages in my hand cry out that Hector is sinking—is dead—with the bronze spear of Achilles in his throat. Another page—there is a wild shout of triumph from the plain. Achilles, lashing his chariot steeds, dashes past beneath the Scæan Tower, dragging by the heels the stripped and bloody body of my beloved Trojan. Priam, at the agonizing sight, tries to rush out that he might die with his son. Hecuba goes almost mad with grief. Andromache, Hector's wife, tries to throw herself from the walls. Helen, the cool, the imperturbable, must witness this further havoc she has brought to a city. And the war, and the pages, move on.

Achilles' reign of terror is short-lived. A truce is declared, and Paris, coming upon Achilles unarmed, shoots him treacherously with a poisoned arrow in his one vulnerable spot—his heel.

Hector gone, Achilles gone, Ulysses now becomes the dominating figure in the war. His leadership, I know, is destined soon to end the struggle, for the pages of my story are turning fast, and few remain. Few remain, yet what a bloody tale they tell!

They tell that the Greeks, apparently, have raised the siege and gone away, leaving behind the fateful Wooden Horse.

With songs and procession the Trojans roll the strange statue back across the plain, and demolish a section of wall that blocked its triumphant entrance —and night comes—and Troy is drunk with revelry.

It is too dark to read. I toss my book aside. The sun has gone down behind the island of Imbros in whose shadow the Greek fleet is hiding. I know it is hiding there. I have known it for twenty years. I know that the Wooden Horse is a clever stratagem of Ulysses; that Ulysses himself is hidden inside along with a score more of daring Greeks. I do not need my book to tell me of all the fury that is to be let loose before the night is gone. I stand upon my Scæan Tower, and breathlessly wait for the storm to break.

Behind me the Trojans, completely occupied with feasting, are not aware that Ulysses and his followers are stealthily emerging from the horse. Before me through the starlight the Greek army, returned from Imbros, is stealing across the plain and up to the gates of the doomed city. Quietly, cautiously, they are massing in deep ranks below the Scæan Tower.

There is a stifled cry in the darkness below. Ulysses has run his sword through the Trojan sentry. Groaning slowly the gates open. The Greeks rush in. There are shouts everywhere, and slaughter. The city is helpless; no one is spared. In the midst of the carnage King Priam hurls a feeble spear at Pyrrhus, Achilles' son, and invites his own destruction.

Helen, more beautiful than ever, awaits the end serenely. Menelaus seeks her out, determined to satisfy his ten years' hate and his honor as an outraged husband and king. But when he finds her, she is still so fair, still so much the woman he has loved, that he flings away his sword (somewhat to Helen's disgust) and kneels in homage at her feet—while all outside the streets run with blood, and the red fires mount to the heavens, and Troy becomes a smoking shell of ruins.

Ruins, yes,—immortal ruins. Not for three thousand years has a day passed but some Greek, or Roman, or Byzantine, or modern Occidental has dreamed of Troy, or read of Troy, or gone to Troy. Its fame is imperishable; its romance is inexhaustible. To our own far-away new world its great name has echoed, and I, for one, am proud to have answered its calling, to have lain atop the crumbling battlements in the twilight with the wind whimpering fretfully through the grass-grown ruins, and with the ghosts of Priam and Hecuba, Helen and Andromache drifting

beside me, as each night they mount to the Scæan
Tower to watch, with hollow anguished eyes, the
ghostly horses of the ghostly Achilles dragging
Hector's shadowy body before the silent, sleeping,
sorrow-laden mound that once was Troy.

## LOTUS LAND

# CHAPTER XI

## LOTUS LAND

ULYSSES was almost the last chieftain to leave the Trojan shores with his remaining command of men. His successful stratagem with the Wooden Horse had increased his already great prestige so enormously that even Agamemnon came to consider him the wisest and ablest of all the Greek captains, and requested his services in the difficult task of demobilizing the spoil-laden army.

Increasingly restless from this delay, Ulysses and his twelve ships at last set sail for Ithaca. To reach this island it was necessary to voyage six hundred miles, traverse the entire length of the Ægean, double the southernmost point of Greece where Cape Malea looks out upon the southern sea, and then turning north sail far up the west coast of Greece.

Each ship had held a hundred men ten years before when they came to the wars of Troy. Scarcely half as many were returning, for the Ithacans had always been in the thickest of the fight, and the Trojan arms had wrought destruction in their ranks.

This remnant of six hundred was further diminished by fighting on the Thracian coast where Ulysses landed his men to sack the city of the Ciconians who had been allies of Troy during the war.

Leaving behind seventy more men, dead or captured, he set out again, and, favored by wind and wave, scudded past Lemnos, past the familiar shores of Skyros (what tragedies had come to pass since Ulysses had first set foot ten years before upon that little isle!), past Delos, past Milos. The war-worn soldiers paid small heed to these romantic islands. They were too eager for Ithaca.

The southern course was ended, Cape Malea was rounded, and all was going well. The helmsmen joyfully turned the prows of the twelve ships to the north into their own Ionian waters.

But alas! The offerings to propitiate the gods for a safe and quick return were evidently not sufficient, for none other than Ulysses himself was destined ever to reach Ithaca.

Scarcely had the last ship passed the cape when heavy currents began to resist them, and the north wind, sweeping down the Ionian Sea, blew so fiercely that they were driven helplessly before it, far out into the boundless Mediterranean. Seven days, eight days, nine days, they were sped southwestward, cursing the perverse winds and this further delay in their home-coming.

On the tenth day in utter ignorance of their location, they sighted a great verdant island with palm-
trees reaching out from the shore.  To the weary
Greeks this meant fresh water, a cool refuge from
the sun and an escape from the tossing sea.

As they drew closer, a deep curve in the shore and
a glittering white beach indicated a safe haven.  Impatiently they turned their ships toward it.  With
one final stroke of the oars, the twelve ships were
driven high upon the sands of the harbor,—the harbor
of modern Houmt Souk, the little metropolis of the
island of Jerba which now belongs to the French
colony of Tunis and is located just off the African
coast not far from the line that divides Tunis from
Italian Tripoli.

To investigate what manner of people lived here
Ulysses sent out three of his men.  Straightway they
found a road, leading, beneath a great aisle of waving
palm-trees, from the beach to a village.  Never had
they seen such a luxuriant land.  The flowers, the
ferns, the soft, moist, musical wind would have been
acceptable to any traveler, but to the Greeks who had
endured the past ten painful years in a barren military
camp, this lush tropical garden seemed like the
Elysian Fields.  I know, because I, too, went there
straight from Troy.

Ulysses' men came at length to the settlement
half hidden beneath hibiscus trees with their flaming

blossoms and palms heavy with dates.  They met the residents there, and found that they were a mild-eyed, melancholy, hospitable people who lived upon a honey-sweet fruit.  The Greeks were cordially received and fed this flowery food, which they learned was called the lotus.  "Now whosoever of them did eat of it had no more wish to bring tidings, nor to come back but there he chose to abide with the lotus-eating men, ever feeding on the lotus, and forgetful of his homeward way."  To all of Ulysses' men who tasted of this enchanted fruit,

> "Most weary seem'd the sea, weary the oar,
> Weary the wandering fields of barren foam.
> Then some one said, 'We will return no more.
> Hateful is the dark-blue sky,
> Vaulted o'er the dark-blue sea.
> Death is the end of life; ah, why
> Should life all labor be?
> Surely, surely, slumber is more sweet than toil,
>     the shore
> Than labor in the deep mid-ocean, wind and wave
>     and oar;
> O, rest ye, brother mariners, we will not wander
>     more."

Still on top the Scæan Tower, Roderic woke up the morning after the fall of Troy, with a yawn.  "Tennyson was right, Dick:—'Surely, surely, slumber is more sweet than toil.'"

"*I* should say it is, thou sluggard. *I* was up at

sunrise to find if anything was left of the Trojans. Nothing is. They're all dead and the Greeks are all gone. There's not one in sight even on the beach. I've been out to see if they left anything for our breakfast. Behold! One watermelon, one armful of bread, one pocketful of cheese. And what's more, I've engaged two horses with lovely wooden saddles to take us back to Abydos. I know having to get up and eat cheese is an awful hardship, but you'll recuperate when we get to Africa."

We walked the last few of the twenty miles to the Byron House (I suspect Byron, who likewise rode back from Troy, did too, if he had a saddle like ours) and that night on a steamer were once more in pursuit of Ulysses. No ship plied from the Hellespont to Jerba; so we had to return to Athens to look for further transportation.

As ill luck fell upon Ulysses on leaving Troy, likewise did ill luck fall upon me. Awaiting Roderic at Athens were cablegrams calling him home—after I'd spent weeks training him to put up with my disposition! His loss was a heavy one for me. From the first he had been the steadying, responsible element of our expedition, always good-humored, especially under trying circumstances, always generous, always right. I felt safe to plunge into any caprice no matter how indiscreet, if I knew the cool-headed Roderic was there to see I didn't get hurt.

And so long as I traveled under his watchful eye (as at the Hellespont swim) I never did.

After his departure I wandered about Athens at loose ends, trying to find a boat to Jerba, and not caring much whether I found one or not. At Piræus I interviewed innumerable sailboat captains, trying to persuade them to take me to lotus land. No one would venture the nine hundred miles across the Mediterranean in a small sailing vessel, even though I offered the boat's weight in drachmas. The best thing I could find was a Greek freighter bound for the city of Tunis, from which port I could probably reembark for Jerba. It would take two passengers. I was one.

The other was a prince, not by royal inheritance, but by attributes of mind and heart. A professional German-Swiss ski-master, he spent his winters in the Alps, and his summers wandering about the world with a knapsack swung on one shoulder and a violin on the other. He was twenty-six, a graduate of the University of London where he had been an active Fabian, a brilliant linguist, and a gifted musician. Yet with all this he had deliberately chosen the rugged life and, except for his summer excursions, never left his mountains.

He told me of the exhilarating Alpine winters and of the miles he swiftly traveled on his skis. I told him of my Hellespont adventure and the Odyssey I was attempting to relive. We had several things in common. We both revered Rupert Brooke. We had both swum in Lake Geneva in the shadow of the Castle of Chillon. We had both climbed the Matterhorn to watch the dawn break over the Alps. Here was an intriguing substitute for the sorely-missed Roderic, and he agreed that if I would go with him to Carthage, just outside of Tunis, he would go with me to the lotus land.

We woke up the first morning out, to find to my inexpressible delight that our lumbering freighter was just off Cape Malea, with the island of Cythera close ahead. Over this very spot the twelve ships of Ulysses had sailed. Just as their helmsmen had done, our helmsmen turned us sharply to the west. We cleared the cape, with a strong northeast wind, such as drove the Ithacans to Africa, blowing the smoke from our stack ahead of us. In my mind's eye I could see the Greek crews struggling to hold against the elements, and their despair when they saw Cythera disappearing to the north.

In three days we passed Malta where both Ulysses and I were to come at a later date, and finally into the harbor of Tunis.

I was not at all unwilling to visit Carthage, despite the fact that my labors at Lawrenceville with Virgil's Ænead had not especially endeared me to Dido's capital. After the death of Hector, Æneas had been

the greatest defense of my pet Trojans, and for that
service I was glad that he had escaped here to Carthage after the sack of Troy, although as a man he had
always bored me to death with his monotonous, inces-
sant virtue.

The two-hundred-mile voyage along the Tunisian
coast to Jerba was made painfully in a small sailing
vessel. Leon and I could have covered the distance by
motor in one-tenth of the time, had I not been determined to approach the enchanted island from the sea,
as Ulysses had approached it. True, our craft was
crowded with pigs and cows, which at times got very
obstreperous. To restore order, Leon would unsling
his violin and put them to sleep with *Du bist wie eine
Blume,* and *Stille Nacht, heilige Nacht,* which he sang
divinely. When we weren't clinging to the gunwales
for dear life to keep from being pitched overboard, he
taught me to yodel and smoke hashish. The latter
proved so delightful, I didn't care whether we *ever*
got to Jerba.

But we did. I knew it was lotus land from afar:
the dense fringe of palms silhouetted against the
clouds and the indigo sky, the white ribbon of beach,
the clear green water into whose transparent depths
one could look and see the sandy ocean floor, and the
rainbow sails of the fishing boats, blue, rose, orange,
violet, bobbing in scores over the sponge fields at the
entrance to the harbor. All this told me that here

was the place whose flowers and fruits had seduced
the Greeks so completely that they forgot the world
and wanted only to dream away the rest of their lives
in this enchanted garden.

After seeing Jerba I really didn't blame them.
Leon and I went there planning to stay only two
days ourselves; we stayed twenty, and even then left
with the same reluctance Ulysses' men had shown
three thousand years before.

As our little boat docked at the pier I looked
scrutinizingly at the crowds that watched us land, to
see if they were "mild-eyed and melancholy," and if
they languidly bore the branches of the lotus tree.
Not one of them did. Instead a number of brisk
French customs officials in white uniforms came to
meet us, and, behind them, half a hundred chattering
Arabs who were about as unmelancholy a lot as a
flock of blackbirds. There were color and motion and
life in every direction. Ulysses wouldn't know the
place to-day.

The road, however, to the city of Houmt Souk
has probably changed very little. There are still the
same tall palm-tree lanes, the same hedges of flaming
hibiscus, the same fragrant breeze that never lost its
tang of salt, and the same countless millions of
lavender crocuses that showered the fields like
lavender rain, and hid the earth on every hill and dale
with a blanket of bright lavender.

Ulysses certainly didn't have two French-speaking porters to carry his baggage and escort him to a neat little hotel, as we did, where Madame asked if we would have red wine or white.

That very day was the date of the big monthly fair. The tiny arcade shops were packed with visitors from the hinterland,—tall arrogant Arabs wrapped in unbleached woolen garments, and gliding along in their bright yellow slippers.

In the great square before the mosque, the perishable products of the island were piled in blazing array: baskets of enormous gold pomegranates, tons upon tons of fresh-gathered olives awaiting the auction block and oil press, great branches of rich red dates, little hillocks of bright oranges, huge oily lemons competing with the splash of tangerines for brightest hue.

The piles of octopuses and other piscatorial foods of like strangeness we found on sale reminded us of the brilliant-colored fleets of fishing boats we had seen scouring the sea just outside the Houmt Souk harbor. This looked as if it might be a jolly adventure,—to spend the day in diving for sponges or octopus or whatever it was they went out to get. Our hotel proprietress only said the word and a dozen sailboat owners were at our door ready to accept paying passengers for the day. The price was adjusted by the harbor commissioner, and since the construction of each boat was exactly the same, and the sailing skill of each captain alike unknown to us, the only point left on which to pick our boat was the appeal of its colored sail.

Leon and I carefully looked over the field. All blue sails we eliminated. They were too near the color of the sky. The green ones were not bright enough; the salmon proved a bit dingy on close inspection. Leon at last decided on a brilliant red, while to me the yellow seemed the most alluring. But no, Leon stubbornly clung to red.

"Oh, don't be so selfish," I said to him with some impatience. "The yellow is the much more lively and inspired color. Don't you remember how the yellow sails flashed brightest when we first saw them from across the Bay of Gabes? I *insist* on yellow."

"Don't be so selfish yourself," he retorted. "Red is the great primary color. It's the color of wine and rubies and love and warm lips and blood,—and this is the only sail in the fleet with that color. It's unique; it's distinctive; it shows a soaring imagination."

Neither of us would budge an inch. Then I thought of a magnificent compromise.

"Leon! I have it! Let's take an orange sail. That's red and it's yellow too. It has all the red love and red lemonade and red flannel underwear *et cetera* you demand, and also my yellow sunshine and optimism and gold. That would satisfy everybody."

"Dick, you're a genius."

So we picked out an orange sail that was sponge-gathering on this day and, once more the best of friends, scudded in a ten-foot boat over the white-floored harbor.

About three miles out, the skipper rolled up his sail and cast overboard a metal cylinder with a glass pane in the submerged end. Being water-tight the cylinder sank only about a foot and floated there. It was big enough to receive one's head in the open end. Thus freed from the ripplings and light-reflections on the surface of the water we could see the sponges growing forty feet below on the sandy floor. At this extreme depth the sponges were safe, for the diver who accompanied each boat was never skilful enough to work so far under water, nor was it possible to handle forks of such a clumsy length. In fact the forks were rarely made more than twenty feet long.

At first, though it was easy to see the innumerable fish moving about (and not difficult to drive the sponge-fork into the unsuspecting creatures), I was quite unable to detect the gray green sponge from the rest of the scattered marine life on the bottom. But little by little Leon and I came to recognize them. Sometimes they were a foot across and when logged with water presented a serious weight problem.

Our diver was a lad about eighteen. With a clip

over his nose he would swim to the floor and either tear the sponge loose himself and drag it to the surface, or else, if the water was shallow enough, direct the long fork, held on to from the boat, into the poor sponge's heart.

Leon and I soon had enough of spearing them. We wanted to dive for them, and when Abdulla, the boatman, discerned a fat prize in about twenty-five feet of water, we took off our clothes, put clips on our noses and went after it. I'd never descended into water of more than swimming-pool depth in my life, and didn't know the most elemental rules of "deep" diving. The boy seemed to be as much at home in the cold green depths as the sponges. If he could be, I could be.

Oh, how wrong I was! Before I'd driven myself down fifteen feet, the pressure on my lungs and heart became so painful, I came scrambling back to the surface half-suffocated and gasping for air. Leon had experienced the same thing. Evidently we couldn't make our living gathering sponges at *this* depth. But we *would* have a sponge even if we had to capture it in the bathtub.

Abdulla was loath to retreat to more shallow fields; the reward there wasn't worth the trouble. We settled that by offering him twice the value of a day's yield in deep water. Being very willing to humor us at this price, he raised the famous orange sail, and

away we sped half the distance to the harbor, not
stopping till we reached ten-foot water.

Here we tried it again, and with better luck. The
sponges thus close to shore were miserable, anemic
little ones, so in order to help out we brought up hand-
fuls of starfish, oysters and sea shells.

We found it great sport, after we became somewhat accustomed to the pressure, snooping over the
ocean floor in these tropical sunshiny waters, meeting
the fish face to face, and getting acquainted with a
beautiful new emerald world we had never known.
After the first day of practise I was able, by breathing deeply several times before submerging, to ravish
a sponge at twenty feet, while Leon took naps on the
ocean floor and decided to give up being a wandering
minstrel and become a mermaid.

For the next two weeks Leon and I wandered
aimlessly about the island, ever charmed by its flaming colors, and its relics of ancient civilization. From
dimmest antiquity it has been a flowering oasis along
the desert coast of Tunis, and every succeeding con-
queror that has flourished in the Mediterranean has
occupied, developed and greatly prized Ulysses' lotus
land.

Twenty miles across, it afforded ample opportunity for excursions. We swayed on camel-back to the
far points of the island, looking for deserted beaches
on which to swim, watching the olives pressed to oil

in crude stone mills a thousand years old, gathering oranges with the hospitable farmers, living on native bread, melons and gigantic pomegranates, idling along the paths under the clouds and the blue African sky, or across the fields which seemed to glow a brighter hue each day with the tidal wave of lavender crocus.

Leon never parted from his violin. He played it in squalid villages where he always collected more children than Hamelin's Pied Piper. He played it on the starlit beach if we stopped there to pass the night. Best of all he played it when we called upor the rural French-conducted schools. Here he completely hypnotized the awed little Arabs with his sunburned smile and his simple German melodies that kept them still as mice. Visitors may come to Jerba, and visitors may go away, but the laughing brown children of this enchanted island will never forget the bronzed, bare-legged man from the far-off world who never grew tired of making sweet dreamy sounds come from his magic bow and box.

And so the slumberous summer days drifted lan-guidly along in this land where it is always afternoon. Whether it was Monday or Friday, June or September, we did not know or care. We had tasted of the lotus, and like Ulysses' men wished no more to roam. Just what Jerban fruit it was that bewitched the Greeks, we do not know. Some say the jujube, once

though no longer, found on Jerba; some say it was
the red dates for which the island is famous, and
which the Greeks, accustomed to a harsh diet of meat
and cereals, found irresistible.  I think that it was no
one of these things, but all; that the "lotus" was just
the general seductiveness of the island.  Certainly the
effect was the same on the Ithacans and on us.

Only by making ourselves a sacred promise that
we would return to Jerba the moment our present
expedition was completed, could we set a date for our
departure,—and that was not to be until the moon,
which had enchanted my Marble Maidens two lunar
months before, and which was now waxing rapidly,
should reach its fulness.

Jealously we watched it grow, until our last night
came.  To-morrow we would turn away and, in
Ulysses' tracks once more, follow him to the Cyclops'
cave.

When the evening was well advanced, Leon took
his violin, and we strolled out into the luminous white-
walled city to find a quiet refuge and to play a sad
farewell to lotus land.

We passed the mosque.  The door was flung wide
open, and the courtyard was deserted.  Ghostly white
in the blue moonlight, the minaret rose above the
trees, above the walls, above all the earth, into the
blue African night and the stars.  Braving the wrath
of Allah we entered the courtyard.  No one chal-

lenged us; so we climbed the ancient circular stair through the impenetrable ink to the muezzin's topmost balcony.

There was the shining Mediterranean over which Ulysses had come and over which he had departed. Inland the spectral olive trees, wave upon wave, dotted the lavender land, and all about us clustered the white, still, starlit city. Leon removed his violin from its battle-scarred case and ran his bow affectionately across the strings.

"What shall I play for you, Dick?"

Any music would have been so painfully beautiful in this high, calm minaret, it did not matter much.

"Do you know the overture from Mendelssohn's *Midsummer Night's Dream?* That's what this evening is, Leon."

He knew it well. Clear and fine, this tintilating, dancing, elfish music floated from our tower, so shy at first the people in the streets below did not know whence it came, or if it came at all. Little by little the violinist took courage, leaned more firmly on his bow, and with increasing resonance poured out the *Dream* into the night. It drifted down into the gardens where the jasmine bloomed; it spread sweetly through the tree-tops, and out into all the air so that whoever breathed it, heard.

Quiet groups began to collect in the streets below. Never in Jerba's history had anything but the

muezzin's call to prayer come from the old minaret,—
and now this intangible, fairy-dance that falls and
falls from the dark tower. They were familiar with
shrill, nasal, Oriental music. But here was something
utterly mystifying and appealing. Houmt Souk
had known few violins, and never had it heard one
played so skilfully—in the starry darkness, from a
source in the high minaret, which they could not see
and could not understand.

For a Jerban to have carried his pipes into the
mosque would have been sacrilege. Yet no one came
to disturb Leon and me. And so in the moonlight,
his violin sang on and on, of triumph, and pain, of
loneliness, and of yearning. Rimsky-Korsakow's
*Song of India* floated away with a dreamy languor
that seemed part of this lotus land. He played the
*Hymn to the Sun* from *Coq d'Or,* and the swelling,
radiant *Prize Song* from *Die Meistersinger.* And
there was Wagner's gentle, muted *Evening Star*
from *Tannhäuser,* and *Prince Igor's* mad ballet.
Unconscious of the realms below, he stood with the
wind from the sea rumpling his hair; his face and
violin lifted toward the pale golden goddess revealing
herself in the high altar of the sky.

It was almost midnight before he thought to pause.
The lights from street and window had faded one by
one, and one by one our audience had faded too.
Leon's fountain of music was running low. There

remained, before we left the old minaret alone with the stars, but one more song to sing:—Tosti's *Good-By*. Lifting his bow one last time, he played the familiar melody, and as he played he spoke the familiar words:

"Hush . . . a voice from far away! . . . 'Listen and learn,' it seems to say. . . . 'All the to-morrows shall be as to-day. . . . all the to-morrows shall be as to-day.' . . . The cord is frayed . . . the cruse is dry . . . the link must break . . . and the lamp must die. . . . Good-by, . . . Jerba, . . . good-by, . . . good-by. . . . Good-by, . . . Jerba, . . . good-by."

Back from across the courtyard of the mosque there came to us one small, sad echo of "Good-by." Then the last faint whisper of harmony died away, and over the land of the lotus there was silence.

# THE CYCLOPS' CAVE

# CHAPTER XII

## THE CYCLOPS' CAVE

ULYSSES did not entice his lotus-loving men away
from Jerba on any such simple pretext as promising
to let them return as soon as they got home. Using
sterner methods he "led them back to the ships weeping, sore against their will, and dragged them beneath the benches, and bound them in the hollow
barques."

We do not know how many days the ships bore
northward seeking again the Ionian Sea and Ithaca.
We only know that after having "sailed onward,
stricken at heart" they bumped at length into Sicily
at its extreme western end just at the point where the
modern city of Trapani is built.* About four miles
offshore, the Greeks noticed a rugged island called
to-day Favignana, and in one of its harbors Ulysses
chose to beach his ships, for the moment, until he could
test the safety of the mainland.

---

*Some traditions place the Cyclops' cave on the east coast of Sicily.
But if this theory is held, Ulysses could not have reached Æolus' island,
his next stop, without going between Scylla and Charybdis.

Next morning, accompanied only by the men sailing in his own ship, he crossed the straits between Favignana and Sicily. When they came to the mainland they noticed a cave on the face of a cliff near the sea. Choosing from his crew the twelve bravest men to follow him, and leaving the others on guard, Ulysses struck out to see who lived there. He carried not only his sword but also a skin of strong wine with which he was prepared to win the heart of any fierce savage he might meet.

They entered the cave and, finding it to be the dwelling of an absent shepherd, decided to wait and see what he was like. Not till evening did he return, and then Ulysses bitterly regretted his curiosity, for the cave owner proved to be not a man like themselves, but the terrifying, one-eyed cannibal giant, Polyphemus.

To follow Ulysses to the Cyclops' cave, Leon and I had to drag ourselves away from Jerba and its enchantments. A storm, which began the day we left, prevented our chartering the little trading vessel that had brought us from Tunis and striking out boldly for Trapani straight across three hundred miles of open Mediterranean in the exact tracks of Ulysses, for the Tunisian captain did not have the courage to put out to sea in heavy weather. In his disappointment Leon would have kidnapped Abdulla and the

orange-sailed sponge boat and crossed to Sicily in
this, but we both realized in time that the precious
violin would probably never live through it.

The only alternative was to return to Tunis by an
un-Homeric motor-car.

We reached the city in time to make a Naples-
bound passenger boat stopping at Trapani. In the
face of ever increasing wind, the ship struggled out of
the harbor into one of the most savage seas I've ever
known. Leon and I thanked our guardian devils that
we had not persevered in the sailboat plan. We
could not have remained afloat an hour, and if we had
we would have been swept hopelessly from our course
to end up in Spain or Palestine.

Next morning, as the ship was plunging past the
rocky coast of Favignana where Ulysses' ships
awaited his return from Polyphemus' cave, we weak
and weary passengers emerged from our cabins more
than willing to disembark at Trapani.

Here we struck the rain which was now accompanying the wide-spread storm. It fell in torrents.
All morning and until early afternoon the blustering
downpour beat at our little hotel. This was a fine
greeting to the Cyclops' land. Even a large bottle
of wine failed to cheer us. It wasn't drunk in vain,
however, for it did make us reckless enough to thumb
our noses at the elements, leave behind the violin and
all our clothes except shirts, shorts and shoes, and.

pretending we were ducks, splash out hatless, rain-coatless, umbrellaless into the flooded streets.

A map gave us the general direction of the Cyclops' cave; we were told at the hotel it was about ten miles up the coast. That seemed rather remote from Favignana. The *Odyssey* reads that when Ulysses on leaving this island "came to the land which *was not far off*, he noticed a cave." But it was no doubt just our wine that made us see incongruities.

Before walking ten feet we were drenched. We didn't care; it was such good sport wading in the pools along the streets and building mud dams across the gutter. We hadn't had so much fun in years. It was still summer, and though the storm had brought a falling temperature, we paddled along fast enough in the blinding rain to keep comfortable in our sodden clothes.

The road presently struck the shore and followed close alongside the roaring breakers. On the other side the western slope of Monte San Giuliano, barren of any habitation and half hidden in clouds, rose abruptly above us. Reckoning after an hour's walk that we were about one-third the way, we sat down on the rail of a bridge to take the gravel out of our shoes. Looking about at the dripping scenery we caught sight of a low-browed cavity in the hillside about two hundred yards from the road.

"Let's go over there and wait for the rain to stop."

I said to Leon. "I'm beginning to get cold already
and we've still a long way to walk."

He was more than agreeable. As we approached
what we thought was only a cavity, we saw that it was
a cave, and a rather large one. We heard the bleating of sheep inside, and saw smoke coming from the
entrance. Leon hallooed as we came up to it. Two
angry dogs ran out to bark at us, and a voice from
within called them back. We entered through a gap
in a five-foot stone fold, and found ourselves in a
wide-spreading grotto fifty feet square, thirty feet
high, and packed with sheep driven there to escape
the storm. On a ledge, drying his blanket before a
charcoal fire, the shepherd himself sat, a piquant-
faced, weatherbeaten, tousle-haired, barefooted
Sicilian boy about fifteen (a slightly larger edition of
Lazarus), puffing solemnly away at a cigarette.

My Italian was mostly French, so Leon, who
seemed to speak every language on earth, had to do
the saluting and felicitating. The lad's dialect, if
difficult, was understandable.

"We'd like to rest here from the rain, if we may."

"Come in, Signors."

The young shepherd received us with an uncon-
cerned air that made him rather likable.

"It's a fine cave. Do you own it?"

"No, nobody owns it. I spend the nights here in
summer. The wall there keeps my sheep in."

"Σ our cave doesn't seem to be marked on my map. Has it a name?"

"Ah, *si, si*.  It is *La Grotta di Polifemo!*"

The young Cyclops peered at us quizzically and no doubt wondered what on earth had struck us that we should be jumping up and down so at the mere mention of the cavern's name.

"But Leon," I said skeptically, "this can't be the grotto.  The hotel people said sixteen kilometers— that's ten miles—and we've come scarcely four. Maybe they were just frightening us into hiring one of the hotel motors.  Still, Polyphemus might have had two grottos.  Ask the boy."

The shepherd insisted this was the only one he knew about.  We asked him if his name was Polyphemus Junior.  He said no, that it was Rosario.

Not at all disappointed by this unexpected discovery of our destination, Leon and I sat down to rest and to decide what to do next.  We decided the best thing to do next was to take off our clammy shirts and shorts, and dry them before the shepherd's fire.  It was a slow process for the fire was only a handful of charcoal, and the air was heavy with moisture.  We might have been a bit miserable except for Rosario's cigarettes which he shared with us like a true host.

By the time our clothes were dry, twilight had come, and with it yet more tempestuous winds and heavier downpour.  The shepherd milked several of his goats and gave us a full pail to drink along with a portion of his bread and cheese. The night grew darker—the rain, rain, rain, fell incessantly. Presently there was no light left in the cave except the glowing coals, and our cigarettes, and the flashes of lightning. The five of us (two men, one boy, and two dogs) were sitting close together for companionship against the storm and the darkness and the weird unfathomable shadows that filled the deep cavern. Whatever natural self-consciousness the boy may have felt on his meeting with two foreign strangers, he had lost by now and talked with less shyness than one might have expected.

"Do you know why your cave is called La Grotta di Polifemo?" Leon asked him after he had told us simply and ingenuously about his small world.

"Yes. It is because a giant by that name lived here."

"Do you know the story about him?"

The young Cyclops shook his head.

It seemed a shame that this lad who sat where Polyphemus sat, and milked his goats, and tended his sheep, and trod the same hillside, and lived the same life in the same cave as Polyphemus, should not be aware of his infamous predecessor's history, and that this rude sheepfold where he spent his summer nights was one of the most celebrated corners in literature.

So Leon told the boy the story (with such vivid

pantomime that I, knowing it by heart already, followed the narrative as easily as if I'd understood
Italian). He explained briefly who Ulysses was, told
of his landing on the beach below us and his visit with
twelve men to this very cave.

"They came right through this opening," Leon
continued, pointing to the passage between the walls
of the sheepfold. "The cave doorway was much
narrower then. Otherwise everything is just as
Ulysses found it. Nobody was here to greet them
for Polyphemus was away in the pastures up above
on Monte San Giuliano.

"Ulysses' men begged him not to stay here. They
sensed danger. But Ulysses wanted to see what
manner of host this cave dweller might be, so he
made them stay."

The boy was listening eagerly, for Leon was a
master story-teller who relived every small incident of
the narrative and pointed out in the ghostly cavern
every exact spot where events took place. The
shepherd no longer was aware of the rain which the
gusts of occasional wind blew under the ledge in upon
us. He ignored the thunder and his bleating sheep.
He was such a lonely boy—only his flocks for company—so hungry for human association—and here
was some one who had just dropped with the rain
from the clouds to talk to him and tell him stories
about the very roof above his head. His eyes said
eloquently, "Go on!"

"That evening Polyphemus came home, an enormous giant as high as this grotto, and with only one eye in the middle of his forehead. He had a rather quaint way of greeting his guests. He seized two of them in his enormous hands and dashed them on to the floor right here below us, so savagely that their brains flowed forth on the ground. Then he ate them." Leon reenacted dramatically how hard the helpless Greeks were smashed on the rocks.

"Ulysses realized that unless he acted quickly the ogre would destroy them all. He thought of a desperate plan. The wine they had brought along he knew was very strong. He persuaded Polyphemus to taste it, and it was so good that the Cyclops drank the entire skin,—straightway falling into a drunken stupor.

"Acting quickly with four of his men, Ulysses thrust a pole into the fire and when it was red-hot they drove the sharp end of the glowing bar into the prostrate monster's single eye, gave it an heroic twist and ran like mad.'

Leon went through all the motions of the terrible thrust, and the leap to safety, indicating the very recess where the brave Greeks sought refuge. We were all so preoccupied with the story, no one thought to fan the coals so that the raconteur was talking in almost total darkness. But one did not need to see Rosario to know that he was listening with painful

intentness.  When we had built up the fire again,
Leon continued:

"With a yell that could be heard for kilometers,
Polyphemus sprang to his feet, tearing the stake from
his sizzling eye-socket and crying out to Neptune,
his father, to help him lay hands on his tormentors.
He pushed the boulder from the entrance and sat
before it stretching forth his hands to grasp the
Ithacans if they sought to go out along with the
sheep.

"Once more the crafty Ulysses was more than
equal to the situation.  Noiselessly he secured himself and all his men under the bellies of the rams, and
in this way they escaped, for Polyphemus never
thought to look *under* his sheep as they ran past.

"Once the Greeks had put to sea again, Ulysses
could not resist the temptation to taunt his blinded
victim.  With a great mocking shout he hurled deri-
sion at Polyphemus, still watchfully waiting right
here in the cave: 'Hear, Cyclops!  If any man ask
who blinded thee, say that it was the warrior Ulysses
who lives in Ithaca.'

"Of course you or I couldn't shout that far.
Ulysses could, though, because he had a tremendous
voice that easily carried from the sea up here.

"When the Cyclops learned that his enemies had
escaped, he flew into such a rage that he broke off
the top of a hill—I don't know which one, perhaps it

was just the great rock that blocked the entrance, because it isn't here any more—and hurled it at the taunting voice. The huge missile missed the ship by only a hair's breadth and sank thunderously into the sea. You know the little island out there, Rosario, called the 'Asinelli'?"

"*Si, si, Signor*," the shepherd replied with eager understanding. "Is that the rock Polyphemus threw at them?"

"That's the very same rock, Rosario. So you can see how enormous Polyphemus must have been to throw a whole island that far."

"What happened to him then?" The boy's eyes were wide, and so very serious.

"Oh, no one knows. He just disappeared. But I wouldn't be surprised if he came back here some day to visit his old cave. He was the son of Neptune, the sea god, and so he's probably an immortal and still alive. Even Neptune couldn't cure his blindness; so if he comes back to look for his cave, he may have trouble finding it."

"I'll show him the way," Rosario said a little wistfully.

Faintly the dying embers cast a last red glow upon the cavern walls. The rain, rain, rain, and the wind, and the inky night beat across the cavern face. Outside the world was all hostility and sorrow. Inside there was trust, and security from every harm.

Little by little the five of us sank to sleep upon our
rocky beds, disturbed only by the shepherd dogs
which stirred and whined, whenever the ghosts of the
Greeks Polyphemus had eaten drifted forth from
the shadows, weeping and yearning for Ithaca.

# CHAPTER XIII

## STROMBOLI—THE ISLAND OF ÆOLUS

I WONDER why it is that islands charm us so? I suppose it's because we always expect to find romance there,—and so often do. Homer was no less affected by their lure than any one else, and whenever it was possible he made his characters live, or his action take place, on islands. This "blind old man of Scio's rocky isle" was probably an islander himself. The lotus-eaters' island, the islands of Circe and the Sirens; the "Island of the Sun"; Calypso's isle; Scheria, the island home of Princess Nausicaa, and finally Ithaca show how frequently in the *Odyssey* the poet depended on the veil of romance that enshrouds an island to help enchant his audience.

On the most extraordinary island in the Mediterranean, Stromboli,—"a floating island, all about which is a wall of bronze unbroken, with the cliff running up sheer from the sea,"—Homer enthroned Æolus, the king of the winds. And thither, after the escape from the Cyclops, he sent Ulysses with his ships.

Had Ulysses followed the southern coast to Sicily, on leaving Favignana, he might have sailed straight to Ithaca without meeting a single obstacle. But that was not his fate. The winds blew him around the northwest corner of Sicily, and then one hundred and sixty miles eastward. If it was fair weather he saw Æolus' island long before he got there, for it seems to "float" on the horizon, and rises like a smaller Fujiyama in a perfectly shaped volcanic cone three thousand feet high.

All day it pours out its column of smoke from its crater, the cage of the winds; all night with a thunder- ing roar it tosses up great geysers of sparks and bubbles of flaming lava which burst high in the air and cascade in a burning curtain down "the cliff which runs up sheer from the sea."

The ancients never doubted that this roaring, smoking, "floating" island was the home of Æolus and his wind-cages, nor do I doubt it, nor would any one else doubt it who had seen from afar the wild weather-vane of smoke issuing from its rumbling crater, shifting now to the south, now to the east, as Æolus unleashes Boreas to churn the seas with icy tempests, or Zephyrus to lull them again with a gentle western breeze.

With his family of six sons and six daughters, Æolus entertained the weary Greeks for a whole month, and when they sought aid of him for their homeward way, he gave it cheerfully. To Ulysses he gave a sack made from the skin of an ox, and in it he bound all the winds but Zephyrus. Only the West Wind he sent forth to blow them home.

All went well till the Greeks were in sight of Ithaca. Then curiosity as to what was in the leather sack overcame them. They opened it, and out rushed the imprisoned winds which straightway blew the ship back to Father Æolus, back to the cages in the crater of Stromboli.

But this time the King, who had previously been the most obliging of hosts, drove them away, saying: "Begone! I dare not shelter him whom the gods hate; and hated by them thou surely art."

So Ulysses and his men, despairing, launched their weary ships once more, and sadly sailed away from Stromboli.

Leon and I impatiently sailed toward it. As one sees smoking Vesuvius from across the Bay of Naples when the low-lying fog has hidden its link with earth, or Fujiyama from a hundred miles at sea when only its snowy summit hangs suspended in the heavens, Leon and I saw Æolus' island, from far, far off. A haze hung over the ocean, but Stromboli, gleaming in the sunset, poked its steep-sloped cone imperiously above the miserable mist, a "floating" island, a regal, earth-shaking volcano, a glorious picture of grace and symmetry, a perfect thing.

Zephyrus was unleashed, for the weather-vane of smoke was drifting straight toward the east and Italy. However, we did not need Stromboli's weather-vane to tell us the west wind was a-blowing, for in our fishing smack we were being sped forward by it at a spirited rate. We had chartered the boat at Trapani, after the storm had passed, and by heavy bribery prevailed upon the captain and his crew (one man) to make the longest voyage in their lives.

Leon united with his violin and knapsack once more, and I with my camera and baggage (which consisted mostly of some eight different translations of the *Odyssey,* and every learned commentary about it I could find, and a tooth-brush), we sailed away from Cyclops-land, not without first seeing that the hospitable Rosario was provided with a mandolin, a raincoat and enough cigarettes to last him six months.

The same wind that blew Ulysses' ship around the northwest cape of Sicily, blew us too. The sea was still tossing from the storm; the waves frequently slammed over us, but with bailing and praying and clinging to the shore, we made the seventy-five miles to Palermo in thirty hours. I'd never sailed at night before in a small sailboat in the open sea. It was a vivid intense adventure. We were right in the path of shipping and had to watch sharp since both freighters and liners passed us every hour on their way to Africa.

Putting in at Palermo for recuperation we set sail again, and still favored by a bright September sun and the kindly Zephyrus, coasted on east, past the city of the Læstrygones where Ulysses lost eleven of his twelve ships soon after leaving King Æolus. Reaching the Milazzo peninsula, some hundred miles on down the shore, we turned away from the mainland at right angles and sailed straight for the seven Æolian Islands (one for Æolus and one for each of his six sons), the outermost of which is Stromboli, the prison of the winds.

Just as it had called to Ulysses an entire day before he reached it, the mountain called to us, challengingly from afar: "Turn your eyes and your helm to me, mariners. Behold my purple symmetry blocking out the sky. Come climb, climb my roaring, shaking, untrodden slopes; stand at the rim of my thundering crater and watch all the elements of hell hurled into the air. Hear the winds burst from my subterranean cages and fly away in clouds of smoke to Æolus' bidding. Dodge my rain of sizzling stones, breathe my poisonous sulphur breath, flounder in my dense ash banks. Climb me if you dare, you insignificant little worms. But be warned: I shall fight you, and flay you, and if I can, destroy you, for I am a tyrant; I am the merciless master of the storms; I, I, am Stromboli."

The challenge was a visual challenge from the

distance; it was a spoken challenge as we ap‹
proached,—a roar—a concussion— a shaking of land
and sea.  Close beneath the cliff down which the burning rocks and lava tumble, we drove our little boat.
The deep muffled thunder never ceased.  Five times
an hour with mechanical regularity the Old Faithful
of volcanoes roared like a thousand angry lions and,
shooting its shower of blazing infernals a thousand
feet into the air, literally "blew up."

One of these explosions greeted us as we beached
our boat just at darkness on the shore along which the
little town of San Vincenzo struggles, shrinking as
far away as possible from the bellowing crater; another rattled the window-panes as we entered the
small and ancient hostelry, and all through the night
sleep was murdered, for Leon and I did nothing but
lie awake with taut nerves, waiting for the next earthquake, which always made us uncomfortable enough
when it came, and twice as uncomfortable when it
didn't.

Unable to sleep, we got our clothes back on, roused
our grumbling "crew," launched our smack in the
darkness, and with sail and oars circuited the shore
till we could stand just off the two-thousand-foot
terrace down which the volcanic discharge tumbles.

When we reached this point the "crew" stopped
grumbling, and so did our captain.  Neither of them
had ever seen anything so spectacular, and never had

Leon, and never had I. Every twelve minutes the
white hot bubbling lava was shot upward into the
black night amid great fountains of sparks that illumi-
nated heaven and earth with their blazing. Then the
flaming geyser would fall back on to the slope, and
in waves upon waves of molten rock ripple glitter-
ingly two thousand feet down to the hissing sea. The
more solid masses not rolled, but leaped, in a few wild
bouncing plunges, leaving a trail of sky-rockets and
little meteors behind them, and fell thundering into
the water. The crater boomed unceasingly, the terrace flashed and flamed. For ten eruptions—two
hours—we sat in our boat, a hundred yards offshore,
and marveled each time the more at this brilliant,
blazing waterfall of fire.

Next morning dense clouds of smoke hid Strom·
boli's crest, and the natives insisted it was exceedingly
dangerous to attempt the ascent in these circumstances. There was absolutely no trail, and the
whole top of the mountain was a mass of chasms and
old craters and treacherous ash banks which one could
not see for the dense black fog. No one ever climbed
the volcano anyway, even in windy weather when the
smoke was carried aside. Now, there was not enough
wind to remove it; and the thundering devil was roaring and spouting more savagely lately than it had
done in years. Weren't we close enough to the awful
noise here in San Vincenzo? If we went up there the

falling rocks would surely crack our heads; the sulphur fumes would suffocate us. Another deluge of lava over the whole island might be expected any hour; we couldn't choose a worse time to visit the crest, and if we *would* go we were just plain crazy and they washed their hands of us.

But we *would* go. What could be better fortune than to have the volcano perform all its wildest tricks now that we had come so far to see it? The more blood-curdling the San Vincentians (not five of whom had ever climbed the irascible mountain they lived on) painted the terrors of the top, the more alluring it became. However, their warning was *so* dire, Leon and I decided to wait one more day in hope that the summit atmosphere would clarify. At two o'clock that very afternoon we glanced toward the peak,—and the cloud had gone. While it was too late to ascend now, to-morrow morning we would be ready.

To-morrow morning found the sulphur blanket hanging thicker than ever over the crater, only to drift aside at two o'clock again.

"It's like that at this season," said the old lady in whose house we were lodged. "At two o'clock the fog generally lifts."

On the third morning we decided to take a chance on her weather prophecy, and trust to luck that at the same hour the breeze would drive the cloud aside.

By heavy bribery we persuaded one of the stouter hearts to go along (not that he had ever been before) to act as beast of burden. Then having followed the shore to the slope right alongside the escarpment down which the volcanic discharge flowed, we started up,—up through the exuberant underbrush. Halfway we struck the barren slopes of ash and sank into it over our ankles, struggling forward, sliding back. The smoke had drifted half-way down,—dense, suffocating, sulphuric smoke. The roar of each eruption grew more fearful. The rumble of the fiery chunks of lava bounding down the great cascade close beside us grew more disconcerting, especially as we couldn't see it. Each convulsion above left us deafened, and faint inside. The trembling of the mountain caused a sickening feeling of helplessness, and the heavy smoke screen only added to our insecurity.

Our native escort began to climb with less and less enthusiasm, until finally, when the volcano gave a super-terrifying bellow that shook our very teeth, the life-long resident on Stromboli's slopes cried out like a suddenly frightened child, and, with all our water and provisions, fled back down the slope, heedless of the mockery we shouted after him.

The mockery was purely to bolster up our own faint-heartedness. Had either of us been alone, Leon or I would probably have retreated too. But together we had developed a common courage that steadied

our knees when the Æolian thunder broke over our
heads.

It was shortly necessary to make a mask of our
bandanas, for the sulphur fumes and fine flying ashes
were suffocating.  Crawling on upward with utmost
caution we gained the level of the wild furnace, still
invisible.  The soldiers at the Marne could not have
suffered a more terrific cannonading than we when
the hell-hole "blew off" at this close proximity.  It
was enough to give one shell-shock.

Hurrying on as fast as we dared in order to get
as high above the monster as possible before it
bellowed again, we presently noticed that the slope
had flattened out—we must be on the crater rim.
Now precaution was trebly imperative.  We had
absolutely no idea of the summit topography, but that
there were crevices and cliffs and chasms, and somewhere perilously near by a great yawning crater six
hundred feet deep at the bottom of which were several
lava-spouting entrances to the infernal regions, we
knew, though we could not see ten feet ahead.

I looked through the sulphur smoke at Leon's
half-masked face.  Though it was blackened with
lava dust, his ash-rimmed eyes were still twinkling.

"Oh, this lovely mountain air!" he coughed out.
"If Æolus and his six sons and six daughters had their
palace up here, I'll bet they all died of galloping
tuberculosis."

"They certainly would have had to spend their
lives in a bathtub unless they wanted to look as
Nubian as you do, Leon. Maybe they were black
already and didn't mind. I'm not surprised Ulysses
wailed the way he did when the winds drove him back
to this ash-pile."

"Wish I had a drink of water," Leon said abruptly
through his bandana, expressing the thought that was
dominating both our minds.

"Why be so plebeian? I'd much rather have a mint
julep, or champagne in a bucket of ice. They're
just as easy to wish for as water. *My* wish is that
Æolus would chase this cursed cloud away. We're
going to step off into some roaring crater and drown
in a puddle of lava, if he doesn't."

"You make your wishes very timely," said Leon,
looking at his watch. "It's almost two o'clock. I
suggest we sit tight and wait. The weather is exactly
as it was yesterday."

We had not been seated very long when the
earnestly hoped for, and fully expected, relief came.
Gradually the smoke began to drift aside. Eurus
had been sent to our rescue. Thinner and thinner
grew the sulphur fog. We could see twenty feet
away—fifty—a hundred—until presently, though the
cloud was never entirely dispersed nor our vision entirely clear, since there was a continual discharge from
below, the great crater of Stromboli, deep, savage,

awesome, hideously scarred by fire and battle, yawned
wide open beneath our feet.

And as it opened it began to roar its earth-shaking
roar, first deep down below the sea, an ugly ominous
rumble; nearer and nearer it came, fiercer and fiercer.
Then with a concussion that almost knocked us over,
from six hundred feet above it we saw the eruption explode through a huge beehive, hurl its bursting
flaming lava-bubbles up, up, up, toward us as we
looked down upon it, nor spend its force till the high
flung rocks were level with our eyes. The dense thousand-foot column of black smoke that followed
floated on skyward and westward to form the
weather-vane we had first seen sixty miles away, and
the lava fell back upon the slope to tumble down to
the sea in the waterfall of fire we had watched the
night before.

Startled and frightened by these sudden, simulta-
neous dramatics, we caught our breath. All the con-
figuration of the mountain that had puzzled us so
in the smoke, was now completely revealed. The
wall of the great crater was only three-fourths there.
One entire quarter section had been blown out eons
ago, and through the outer edge of its jagged stump,
right at the surface of the mountain, the beehive which
caused the frightful thunder and poured its eruption
down the slope, had broken out. There were a dozen
other minor craters in the big crater floor. Each one

boiled and bellowed, but it was only the beehive
through which all the suppressed steam and smoke
of all the earth's interior seemed to find its deafening
escape.

For an hour we stood on the rim of this amazing
spectacle, with the sea shimmering in a perfect circle,
three thousand feet below, dotted with the six islands
that belonged to Æolus' six sons. Only Mount
Ætna, seventy miles away, broke the hazy horizon.
Five times, while we rested, the beehive "blew off."
Leon and I were suffering terribly from thirst, but
the fascination of watching the geysers of lava, hurled
up from below almost, yet not quite, into our laps,
was so great that we just sat and endured and gloried
in the wildness and brutality of the sight.

The roaring, the bursting, the flames, the inspired
feeling of height and mastery over land and sea, made
an insane something in my brain struggle for expression,—a shrill savage intoxication, a kind of delirium
such as whole armies have in blind, murderous, hand-
to-hand fighting, when killing becomes a lust and a
joy. I wanted to shout back at this roaring thing;
I wanted to fling rocks at the rocks it flung at me; I
wanted wings with which to leap into the abyss and
jeer at the devils as they snatched at me through
these doors to hell. I knew exactly how Nero felt
when he burned Rome for musical inspiration. How
gloriously and wildly he must have played, gone mad

and drunk on the fire below him! Wild music, that
was what I wanted—music as wild and drunk and
savage as this roaring, evil monster.

"Leon, Leon," I exclaimed with arms flung
dramatically out over the chasm, "why didn't you
bring your violin? I want music—*music*, while
Stromboli burns."

Leon answered me with a mock exaggerated calmness such as one uses on a maniac when trying to get
him quietly back into his strait-jacket without his
killing anybody.

"There, there now, Dickie. Don't you get excited.
I'll go back and fetch you the fiddle. And of course
you would need accompaniment,—that would make
it sound much louder,—so I'll bring along a grand
piano. I'll tell you what! You come too and help
me. I'm sure it would be easier to carry if you gave
me a hand."

Leon took me coaxingly by the arm, fearing that
if he used force it would make me suspicious and
rebellious, and I followed happily and submissively
at this delightful idiot's heels, all the way home.

# CIRCE THE ENCHANTRESS

# CHAPTER XIV

## CIRCE THE ENCHANTRESS

HER name was Rosa, and her eyes were black as midnight. We called her Circe because she lived on Circe's lsland—and was an enchantress. Ulysses spent an entire year here with the original goddess; Leon . . . But I'm getting ahead of my story.

Ulysses did not attain Circe's island without suffering the most harrowing difficulties. On leaving Stromboli, the twelve ships of the unhappy Greeks, cast forth by King Æolus, struck Sicily again at the harbor of Cefalu,* the city of the Læstrygones, some thirty-five miles east of Palermo. Here the inhabitants, who turned out to be cannibal giants worse than Polyphemus, cast great stones at every ship that had entered the harbor, so that all but the ship of Ulysses, which had warily remained outside, was destroyed, and their crews speared for food.

All alone the single remaining vessel fled to the northward, one hundred, two hundred, two hundred

---

*Students disagree about the location of Læstrygones' home. Samuel Butler and the city's topography argue eloquently for Cefalu

and fifty miles before they again came to land. This time it was the island of Circe (though at first they did not know it), called to-day Monte Circeo, and located on the west coast of Italy half-way between Rome and Naples. Since the Roman era it has been a rocky promontory rising seventeen hundred feet above the sand-flats that connect it with the mainland. In Homeric times it stood alone in the sea, ten miles from the shore.

Ulysses, having rested on the narrow beach with his demoralized companions, climbed to the top of the steep-sloped mountain to look about. On the opposite side he saw smoke rising from some habitation.

To learn who lived there, one of his lieutenants took twenty-two of the men and found a palace in the woods. On approaching they heard a woman inside, singing with a sweet voice, and plying the loom. Presently, radiant as a goddess, she came out and seeing the Greeks invited them to enter her dwelling, showed the wonderful web she was weaving and gave them wine to drink.

It was fatal refreshment, for their hostess was the enchantress, Circe, and the wine contained mighty drugs which so changed the Greeks that when she touched them with her wand they were instantly changed to pigs. Ulysses would have suffered the same fate himself when he came to investigate, had he not been protected by a certain herb given him by

Hermes to render him immune from Circe's magic.
When her charms failed to work on Ulysses, Circe
realized he was aided by the Olympian gods, and in
alarm not only turned the pigs back to men but
royally entertained the entire company for a year.
Necromancy did not die with Circe, for, just as
the goddess made pigs out of the Greeks, her black-
eyed descendant and disciple, Rosa, made monkeys
out of Leon and me.

We had tarried at San Vincenzo after our conquest of Stromboli just long enough to get clean—
two days. Then launching our fishing smack, we
sailed once more beneath the lava cliff, away from
Æolus' roaring island. As it had bellowed a greeting
to us, it bellowed a farewell and with unexpected
generosity turned its smoking weather-vane to the
south, unleashing a breeze that blew us past the other
islands that belonged to Æolus' sons and safely into
the snug harbor of the Læstrygones.

Ulysses didn't tarry long at Cefalu, and neither
did we, though we had none of the reasons for a pre-
cipitate departure he had. *We* found the Cefalutes
most cordial. In fact after Leon, in a café, played
*Glory, Glory, Hallelujah* on his violin for the assembled multitudes (a hymn he had never heard
before I brought it into his life, and which became
such a favorite with him that I began to regret my
contribution after I'd heard it seven thousand times),

a dozen or more of the younger Læstrygones escorted us all the way to the railroad station.

We had discharged our fishing smack and crew in the harbor, for though Leon and I were willing to risk the long voyage in it across open seas to Circe's island, the captain refused to sail any farther away from his base at Trapani. It was just as well, because had he agreed to go on, this one more time, we'd probably have persuaded him to continue all the way back to Ithaca, and then on home by way of Suez, Singapore, Samoa and San Francisco.

The train took us to Palermo, a ship to Naples, and more trains to Terracina, seventy-five miles up the coast, and the point on the mainland where one takes a vehicle to reach San Felice, the village on the "island" of Circe, ten miles away across the marshes.

San Felice boasts no hotel. No visitors ever come there except crazy archeologists. But Leon and I meant to stay, if not a year like Ulysses, at least several days, and we needed shelter. Leon by now was stony broke; so, not being too fastidious, we walked around the small ill-kept town looking for hospitality.

Passing beneath a balcony where the windows were wide open, we heard a woman "singing in a sweet voice." It was more than a sweet voice: it was a haunting voice. We stopped to listen. She was singing, carelessly to herself as she sat in a chair by the window darning socks.

"There she is," Leon said with a tone of finality.

"There who is?"

"Circe, my child."

"She certainly sings like it."

"And she's weaving a magic web."

"And look, Leon! *There are pigs all around!*"

Hearing conversation below, in a strange tongue, the singer—she was not more than twenty—leaned over the balcony to investigate. We saw her then, clearly, and marveled that so handsome a face and so rich a voice should be found in this savage little village. I suppose Leon and I both stared at her, because she stared back, and smiled, from amusement no doubt at Leon's bare knees. Anyway her smile was divine, and so were her hair and her pale skin, and, as I have said, her eyes were black as midnight.

"Good afternoon, Signorina," Leon said to her in Italian. "We were listening to your singing. It's lovely. Please sing some more."

She laughed shyly, and remained on the balcony.

"We are strangers here, looking for a place to sleep," he continued easily (and I envied him his facile tongue). "There doesn't seem to be any hotel. Do *you* accept lodgers?" he asked with sudden inspiration.

"No-o. But I might."

With a flash of white teeth, and a flash of black eyes, she disappeared with her sock, and returned

with her father, a real man of the soil.  Leon repeated
his request.  There was low consultation between the
two, daughter urging father to oblige us.  No one
could have denied such eyes anything.  So we were
invited in.

"My name is Leon.  His is Riccardo."  My talk-
ative companion believed in getting acquainted at
the start.  "What's yours?"

"Rosa."

Rosa!  It fitted superbly.  She *was* a rose, not of
the frail hothouse variety, but the sturdy bright-
cheeked kind.  There was an air of strength com-
bined with gentleness about her as she busied around
her own room which was being prepared for us,
talking a little timidly to Leon, who gaily talked
back.  Several times she tried to ask me a question
but I was perfectly dumb in the face of her rapid
Italian.  It was exasperating.  I ached to speak her
language,—she was so vital, so good-looking, despite—or because of—her peasant dress and peasant
surroundings.  If I didn't do something quickly to
overcome this confusion of tongues, Leon would
usurp her entire interest.  She was spreading fresh
covers on a bed,—I leaped to help her.  She went out
to the cistern to draw water for our wash-stand,—I
went along and carried the bucket by one side-handle
as she carried it by the other.  The laughter we enjoyed over our struggles to get it up the steps made

us such good friends that when I again faced Leon I gave him a very patronizing look.

At supper—for Leon, backed by Circe's smiling plea, had talked papa into providing us with meals too—I managed to sit next to the enchantress, and we got along famously. Whatever progress I made there, however, was more than counterbalanced after supper by my rival when he took up his violin, and sitting in the open window played *Glory, Glory, Hallelujah* with variations.

Rosa loved music. It was Leon's chief passion. He could follow a song, unknown to him, once, and then play it. Some of Rosa's songs he knew already. A bit self-conscious at first she softly hummed when the violinist struck a familiar melody. Little by little she gained courage, and before our first concert was over was singing with all the abandon of a nightingale,—untaught—unnoticed—unaware of the beauty and rich sympathy of her voice. In the lamplit room, what peasant ruggedness her face might have had was softened away. She sat in the shadows, a picture of pure loveliness. But as she sang she looked at Leon with gentle eyes, and I felt my own cause slipping.

Slipping, yes; but not lost. Next morning I rushed into the battle with a new and telling stroke. I was wearing woolen golf stockings, and they were in shocking state of disrepair. The first time we saw Rosa she was darning socks; so I knew she would know how to darn mine. I reasoned that if I could persuade her to do this for me, all the mother instinct which such an honest-hearted peasant girl as Rosa had in abundance, would be brought out as she saw me standing around helplessly while she darned my stockings. It worked magnificently. She fretted over the disgraceful rips and holes, and while she darned she called me "poor bird" and "poor child." Then and there I resolved to do Penelope's trick and unravel the darning every night so that it would have to be done again next day.

On Sunday the three of us went to the ancient cathedral, Rosa dressed in black, Leon with his knees well laundered, and I attired as foppishly as my wardrobe of one knickerbocker suit and two blue polo shirts would permit. After church we decided to explore the mountain, take Rosa with us as guide, and carry along a picnic basket. Only by subtle maneuvering could I persuade Leon to leave behind his deadly violin.

There was a good path up the back of the mountain to the signal station atop the lower peak. We would have taken this had there not been a fine breeze blowing that day which persuaded us to choose the steeper, pathless, seaward slope, in order to watch the waves dash against the rocks and to visit the grottoes where the Homeric Circe had urged Ulysses to "bestow his goods and all the gear."

Rosa knew every inch of the mountain. It had been her playground as a little girl, so that she had a reverence and affection for it. She knew where the trails were, and the springs, and the ruins. Physical exertion she accepted as a matter of course. She had climbed and toiled like a man, and alongside men, all her twenty years. Monte Circeo offered no difficulties for a girl who had pitched hay and driven oxen. She climbed with as little fatigue as Alpinist Leon himself.

The signal station was attained—twelve hundred feet. It was to this point, probably, that Ulysses came on his reconnoitering expedition, and from here that he noticed the smoke rising from Circe's palace. For us this was not enough. A second peak rose five hundred feet higher, and on top of this were the ruins of Circe's Temple. We decided to spread our picnic lunch on its utmost rock; so, undaunted by the prospect of a yet steeper climb, Rosa found the new trail and led us to the assault.

Such scrambling, such slipping, such shouts of laughter from Rosa! Leon and I both would have been ready to win favor by giving her elaborate assistance, had she not scorned our aid all the way up. On the barren domed summit, the three of us flung ourselves down and let the strong wind cool our faces.

Oh, what a view!—the rolling Mediterranean at our feet on three sides; the mainland of Italy across the marshes; and smoking Vesuvius eighty miles away, beyond the Gulf of Gaeta; and all the rocky islands that are strung along this part of the Italian coast: Ponza and Ischia and Capri. In clearer weather than we enjoyed the sixty-mile-distant dome of St. Peter's itself was visible. While we couldn't see it for the haze, neither could Ulysses.

We used a big stone from the scanty remains of Circe's Temple for a table and made way with the bread and cheese and oranges and wine we had brought along.

Leon told Rosa he thought she was the best sport he had ever seen. I should have had some fine compliments of my own to give her had my Italian not been so elemental. At least Leon didn't have his violin. I'd seen to *that.* The weak point in this little triumph was he really didn't need it, not with his glib tongue and easy sunburned smile. That combination plus the violin was becoming more and more formidable, and I was beginning to be worse than discouraged over the outlook. There they were sitting side by side with their legs swinging over the cliff, chattering away like two magpies, utterly happy and at ease together. Perhaps I'd better do the magnanimous thing, since my case was lost already,—resign in favor of my better equipped rival and reserve my romancing until I either learned to speak more fluent Italian or met some one who spoke English.

Then—just in time—my guardian devil whispered a diabolic suggestion in my ear:

"Remember all's fair in love and war. Leon has his violin and his Italian, but he's stony broke—and *you*—have the money."

"What good will that do, if she likes him better?" I asked hopelessly.

"*What good will that do!* Don't be such a dunce! Isn't she a woman and doesn't she want pretty clothes and junk from the jewelry store? Use your head, son!"

"But I haven't got a lot of money, guardian. I can't give her diamond stomachers."

"Diamond stomachers! Minerva's Owl! All it will take is a string of glass beads to conquer Leon's violin,—and a pair of silk stockings will speak far more eloquently of love than Italian. You'll see!"

Next day the shops were open, and I set out to buy my way into Rosa's heart. The glass beads I found easily,—bright red ones, and the silk stockings also, to match her Sunday dress.

That evening when we went to the cistern in the courtyard for water, I clasped the beads about her neck and had the satisfaction of seeing a perfectly radiant young woman. She danced up the steps with such elation that half the water from the side-handle bucket was spilled back upon me. Had it drowned me, I shouldn't have cared.

At supper I was king. Rosa helped me to the biggest piece of fish and the biggest turnip. Leon seemed very quiet and, the moment our meal was over, pounced upon his violin. This was his irresistible weapon which he wielded against the girl's music-loving nature with a devastating effect he fully appreciated.

He played that night with intense feeling, straight into Rosa's heart. And she sang her lullabies and forgot the red glass beads.

But the silk stockings, so dear to a woman's heart, recaptured my lost prestige. They were the first silk stockings she had ever possessed; and a gift of the Italian crown jewels could not have made her happier. She tried to tell me, by speaking emphatically and with pantomime, how much she thanked me. While I understood the idea, Leon (very bored) had to interpret most of the words.

He met the stocking blow with masterful tactics, taking advantage of his ability as a raconteur and holding Rosa spellbound by telling her of his ski-jumping in the Alps, of the exciting bob-sled races and the mid-winter mountain climbing,—things that this child of sunny Italy had never dreamed of. She listened as eagerly and admiringly as had the young Rosario in the Cyclops' cave, and her opinion of Leon as a sportsman and a hero soared. I had tales to thrill her too,—tales of the Himalayas, and the jungles of

India and Malay, tales of Spain and Siberia, and of
the wonders of America, but not one small adventure
could I relate to Rosa in order to win a part of the
admiration she was heaping upon Leon. And Leon
knew that my pride would not let me use him as an
interpreter to match his tales of prowess, just as his
own pride haughtily refused to borrow money from
me with which to combat my bribery methods. No,
each of us had chosen the weapon he could wield best
under the circumstances, and we felt it dishonorable
to steal the other man's thunder.

So, as Ulysses in the palace of Circe, on this
beautiful mountain-isle, lived on for a year charmed
by the enchantress' voice, her graciousness, her lavish
hospitality, Leon and I put aside all thoughts of
leaving our own Circe's singing and alluring black
eyes. Like Ulysses we were deaf to the call of Ithaca.

The days passed, and the battle raged. I found
for Rosa a pretty box in a notion shop and filled it
with all the moth-eaten confections the town
offered,—and Leon on the starlit balcony played to
her *The Last Rose of Summer*. One afternoon she
danced into our room to show us how beautiful she
looked in a black lace-piece I had given her to wear
on her head,—and Leon straightway broke her heart
with Mendelssohn's *Cradle Song*. After supper that
night I slipped away to buy for my Rosa a privately
owned coral breast-pin that the jewelry-shop keeper

had told me was for sale. But when I brought it home for her I found that she and Leon had gone down to the beach, with the violin,—and they didn't come back for hours.

When Leon tiptoed into our room, close to midnight, and undressed in the dark, I was still awake and spoke to him.

"Hello, Leon. Did you have a good time on the beach?"

"Dick! Are you awake? Yes, it was beautiful. Where did you disappear to after supper? We waited half an hour. You didn't come, so we went ahead. Rosa sang and sang. I'm learning to play her songs rather well. If we keep on, we'll have to go on a concert tour with you as manager."

"I've a better suggestion than that, Leon." An idea had come to me as I lay in the darkness waiting for my friends to return. Deep down in my own heart I realized that I was going to be beaten, that my guardian devil was wrong for once,—partly wrong, at least. With all Rosa's naive susceptibility to pretty baubles, she still loved Leon's music more,— and I knew it. So I magnanimously suggested to Leon that together to-morrow morning we go away from Circe's island.

For a full three minutes he didn't answer. And then he said: "I'll go."

Next morning we broke the news to Rosa. It was

very obvious she was sincerely distressed. As a parting gift I gave her the really fine piece of old Neapolitan coral, bought for her the night before, while she and Leon were singing on the beach. The tears streamed down her cheeks, and she shed a few of them on my coat. Leon was like stone. He didn't say a word of good-by,—just took her hand, and looked at her with his clear blue eyes.

Our inconsiderable board-bill paid to papa, we climbed in the dilapidated motor-bus, and were bumped across the square. Rosa ran behind until we passed through the ancient tower-gate. Then she stood there waving and smiling and weeping, until a turn in the road took us out of sight.

Leon and I knew that the departure from Circe meant our parting from each other. Our voyage northward from Sicily was part of his return journey home to Switzerland. I must go south again to face the Sirens Ulysses had faced, with hope that the gods would see me safely back to Ithaca before the winter came along. At Terracina, on the "mainland," I bought Leon a ticket to Rome (since he was utterly without funds) and one for myself to Naples. He would accept nothing more than the ticket. He was a "wandering minstrel." From Rome he would win his own way with his violin. We parted with heavy hearts. I have never had a more intriguing companion; I have never known a more loyal friend.

A week later at Naples his first letter came to me. It was not from Rome; it was not from Switzerland. *It was from San Felice!*

I opened it with a burning face:

"Odysseus Dick, *Salute!* You probably fell dead when you saw the post-mark on this envelope; so I really needn't write any letter at all. But I'll take a chance that you *did* survive. As you see there's more on Circe's island than a post-marker. I'm here too,—and so is Circe. I'm reoccupying our old room, and writing at the open window before the balcony. Circe is singing in a sweet voice and weaving another magic web. And it's *my* sock this time. I knew I was coming back the minute I agreed to go away, but Rosa didn't know it. I swear that to you. I went to Rome and wired home for money. It came next morning, and that night I was back at San Felice, playing *Glory, Hallelujah* beneath Rosa's balcony. Did she rush out to see me? She did not. She just sat still in the window and sang to my accompaniment. Then we went down to the beach and had a concert.

"I've learned to appreciate your bribery methods, Dick, and brought her a coral necklace from Rome to match your breast-pin. But she still loves the red glass beads the best and wears them all the time.

"To-morrow I'm taking Rosa to Milan. I think she has the finest untrained voice I ever heard, and the teachers there will make a real song-bird out of her. With those eyes, and that smile, and that sympathy of heart, we may some day see our little Rosa queen of La Scala. Then I'm going to write an opera for her and call it *Circe the Enchantress.*"

I found myself sitting in a chair gasping from surprise, and hot from confusion. Those fat rascals!

How completely and how rightly Leon had won the war. Oh well, I didn't care—much. I'd find another—and another, for I knew that

> "Love, like Ulysses,
> Is a wanderer;
> For new fields always
> And new faces yearning . . ."*

And I knew too that I may as well put by any waiting for Rosa, put by my weaving, for

> "Unlike Ulysses,
> Love is unreturning."

---

*From *Ulysses Returns and Other Poems*, by Roselle Mercier Montgomery Copyright, 1925, Brentano's, Inc.

# TO HELL WITH ULYSSES

# CHAPTER XV

## TO HELL WITH ULYSSES

DESPITE this sage philosophy, deep inside I felt dejected and hurt and cheated. I felt that, after all nobody loved me, and decided in this blue mood to go off to the National Museum and eat worms. Maybe I could find a nice ossified one from Pompeii. Anyway the well-known bust of Homer was there, and I thought probably he might like to meet me.

I never did find Homer, but I met Jimmy who was much nearer my age and understood English, which the Greek poet would no doubt have considered a very barbaric tongue. "Jimmy" wasn't her name. I called her Jimmy because her real name was such a preposterous one, and this just suited her.

She was standing all alone looking at some marble god or other, when I first saw her. She seemed vaguely familiar. I wondered if we'd met before.

Everything about her was eloquent of England,— her brogues, her tailored clothes, her ruddy complexion. Her hair was blonde as sunshine—English blonde—and there were several good-natured freckles across her nose.  She looked so breezy and agreeable, and so bored with archeology—and I needed company so badly—that it seemed the most natural thing in the world when I went up and asked her with a perfectly serious face if she didn't want a guide who spoke English and knew all about art.

"Yes," she replied, very much amused, "if you'll promise to make these old fossils interesting."

I promised, and began to conduct her on a tour of the museum in which I had never been before in my life, telling a noble story about each of the master-pieces.

We came to the famous statue of the Drunken Satyr.  "Now this," I enlightened her, "is of partic-ular interest.  It's been used extensively through-out Italy by the Temperance Societies as a symbol. Many of the sober statues got away when the deluge of fire hit Pompeii, but this old boy was so soused he slept through everything and was buried under twenty feet of ashes.  It just goes to show what drink will do for one."

"Funny that's not in the guide-book," my lady said with smiling skepticism.

"Oh, those guide-books are no good.  They always leave out the interesting things.  They don't know anything about art.  Now, just to illustrate, there's not a word in there about this nude Venus."

"What about *her?*" Jimmy asked, her eyes twinkling.

"Why, *she* was found adorning the First Baptist Church. An unusually healthy girl! She weighs one hundred and eighty."

Jimmy couldn't stand my nonsense any longer. She burst out laughing. "I don't think you have recovered *yet* from your Marathon adventure."

"*My Marathon adventure!*" I exclaimed in startled surprise. "How did you know about that? I haven't told a soul."

"Oh, haven't you! You told an entire luncheon table full of people at Athens that 'chivlizhayshun was shaved.'"

"What! You mean you were at Rod Crane's party the day I came dashing in, a bit—er—excited?"

"I certainly was. In fact I left Athens only three weeks ago."

"And you know Rod Crane?"

"Naturally,—having been at his luncheon."

I almost fell on her neck.

"And I'm not at all flattered," she continued, "that you don't remember me. I asked both of you to tea next afternoon. You promised to come and then forgot about it. I met Roderic a few days before his party, in the library of the American Archæology School. I remember he said you had sent him there for enlightenment on the excavations at Troy. I had already seen you several times around town,—always with a red sunburned face and no hat. Roderic told us at the luncheon, just before your arrival from Marathon, that you would probably try to swim the Hellespont next. I saw in the Athens papers later that you had."

"Yes, I remember now. I did think you looked familiar. You must excuse me if I failed to place you exactly. Rod seemed so mortified at my noisy appearance that day, I skipped out to my room with scarcely more than a glance at his guests. But you knew who *I* was all the time I was telling you about art!"

"Of course I did, and I knew you didn't realize I knew. I almost said 'Thank you, Dick Halliburton,' when you offered yourself as guide, but decided that if you wanted to play games I wouldn't spoil it. You should take off your plus-four knickers before you try to be a museum conductor again. You look more like a golf caddie. Where's Roderic?"

"There's no telling. We came back to Athens for a few days from Troy. He had to leave my chaperonage there, and after that he probably went straight to the dogs. I'm all alone; are you?"

"Temporarily. The girl I'm motoring with has gone up to Rome for a week, and left me with the car on my hands. It's parked outside now. If you'd like, we can go for a ride. I've looked so many marble gods in the face, I'm dizzy."

"I'll go along if your car is a Rolls-Royce."

"It is!"

Thus began my friendship with Jimmy. A jollier companion never lived, nor a more energetic one On leaving Greece she had gone by boat to Marseilles. At Nice she had acquired the family chariot, and, accompanied only by her friend, had driven the heavy touring car the entire distance to Naples, seeming to think it not at all remarkable that two *jeunes filles* should be **romping about Italy unescorted.**

Jimmy's tastes were not literary. *Odyssey* was only a vaguely familiar name to her, but she could ride more courageously, swim better, walk farther than any girl I ever knew. I was put to it trying to keep up with this merry young Amazon. She kept me, as her passenger, in a continual state of nervous tension as she drove her motor like mad around the congested environs of Naples, scattering carts and geese and Campanians in all directions. She'd have dashed right up the Matterhorn if it had been in her path. There was no "weaker sex" about Jimmy. She was every bit as self-sufficient as Rod or Leon and was determined to do everything I did on perfectly equal terms.

When I suggested, several days after our meeting, that we climb Vesuvius, immediately she was all enthusiasm.

"Let's go right now," she insisted. "We'll leave

the motor at Resina, at the base, because I want to walk *all* the way up."

Delaying only long enough to get a box of food, we climbed in the car and burned up the highway to Resina, some six miles south of Naples. From here there was a very good road for walking, more than half the distance to the summit. The last third of our path, however, was deep in loose lava-ashes. But after the ascent of Stromboli this had no terrors for me. I had won my Ph. D. in ash-fighting there.

Hot and dusty we reached the crater crest in time to watch the sun set gloriously into the sea. One of the most dramatic pictures in the world spread four thousand feet below us. Far up the Italian coast toward Monte Circeo, we could follow the shore line, and far down the coast, beyond the Sorrento Peninsula, toward Scylla and Charybdis. The lights of Naples were just beginning to twinkle, and the famous Bay, guarded by the islands of Ischia and Capri, was set on fire by the sunset.

Here before us was a wonderfully graphic view of a long and important chapter from my *Odyssey*.

"It's a thrilling moment to me, Jimmy, to sit and look down upon a hundred miles of Ulysses' tracks. His ship skirted the coast as far as we can see. He sailed from the north, hugging the shore, close beside the present harbor of Naples. You've heard of the Sirens?"

"Yes, of course. They were the German blondes who sat on a rock in the Rhine and invited sailors to come on over and get destroyed."

"That's the Lorelei, woman! The Sirens were fatal sea nymphs who lived on some little islands called Li Galli right over there beyond the Sorrento Peninsula,—either there or in the Blue Grotto at Capri. Whichever it was, Ulysses in sailing down the coast had to pass close to them. I'm going to visit both places myself in a few days and you can go along to protect me by your counter-attraction.

"Well, these Sirens were worse than the Lorelei. They sang so sweetly no man could resist them. Ulysses would have jumped overboard just like everybody else if he hadn't been tied to the mast."

"What was he doing so far from home, anyway?"

"He was on his way back to Greece from hell."

"From *what!*"

"Just that. He lived with Circe for a year, and then she sent him straight to hell."

"Was it nagging, or extravagance?"

"Oh, you don't understand, Jimmy. I see I've got to enlighten you in regard to epic poetry as well as art. Give me a cigarette, and be quiet, and I'll tell you just what happened."

Once more I explained who Ulysses was, and roughly sketched his career up to his adventure with Circe.

"You see he had a wife waiting for him in Ithaca all the time he was being entertained by the enchant-ress, but Circe charmed him so with her music and her beauty he fell in love with her, she bore him a son, and he stayed a whole year. He never *would* have gone home if his men hadn't made him. Of course I suspect the woman's everlasting singing was getting on his nerves a bit. At least it would have on mine. Circe was probably very bored too and glad to help him on his homeward way. She told the Greeks that if they wanted to learn what was going to happen to them they'd have to go to hell and con-sult the shade of Teiresias, the prophet. I'd have gone to hell myself from Circe's island, only a month of research in your British Museum failed to locate the place.

"Ulysses had better luck. Blown forward by a wind which Circe provided, he sailed right up to the front door of Hades, and who do you think were the first people he met?"

"Everybody who ever used profanity and played cards on Sunday," Jimmy suggested.

"No sir. The first twelve people he met were *women*," I said gleefully. "Oh, he found some men too. Achilles was there and Agamemnon—his devil of a wife killed him on his return from Troy—and of course Teiresias. The prophet was very obliging and told Ulysses that after great difficulties he would come

to the island of the Sun God—Sicily—where he would
be destitute, and would be tempted to kill the cattle
of the Sun, which grazed there.  If he left the herds
unharmed, he might yet get to Ithaca.  If he
slaughtered them for food, destruction of his ship and
all his men was prophesied.

"Back at Monte Circeo the enchantress gave
Ulysses instructions for the more immediate part of
the journey, telling him about the Sirens, and Scylla
and Charybdis which lay in his path.  Scylla was a
six-armed female monster who leaned out of her cave
overlooking the sea and snatched men up from the
boat decks.  Her cave was on the Italian side of the
Straits of Messina.  Charybdis was a sucking whirlpool on the Sicilian side.  Ulysses must choose to pass
near one or the other, and had better choose Scylla,
because while this way he would lose six men,
Charybdis would destroy his entire ship.

"Here he came down the coast."  I indicated his
route again with my hand in the fast gathering darkness.  "When he got to the point of the Sorrento
Peninsula over there, he put bees' wax in his men's
ears and had them lash him to the mast.  Then he
sailed right under the Sirens' noses."

"What happened?" Jimmy begged.

"Why, they saw his ship coming and put on their
very best record.  They knew Ulysses was a celebrated hero, and were out to hook him.  Nightingales

never sang more sweetly. But they were just wasting their time, for the harder Ulysses struggled to get loose, the tighter his unhearing comrades bound him. It wasn't till the ship was past Amalfi that they set him free. Where are our matches, James? My cigarette's gone out."

"And then what happened? Did Scylla snatch up six of his men?" Jimmy asked, ignoring my request.

"Oh, I forget. I'm tired of talking anyway. Let's eat our sardines, or look at Naples, or hold hands. You and I may as well get acquainted, because we may have to spend the night up here. The cog railroad has stopped running, and we'll never find the path in all this darkness. We can just stay where we are, and watch the fireworks in the crater, and see the sun rise."

"Oh no, we can't, romantic one. If any one learned that I spent the night with you on top Vesuvius, it would simply *ruin* your reputation. And then too, we can't leave Mrs. Rolls-Royce parked too long at Resina. These Neapolitans would steal the paint off."

Jimmy, as usual, had her way. We enjoyed one last long look into the crater, and yawned at the occasional gleam of red light that flared from the cone in the center. After Stromboli's terrible bellowing, Vesuvius' puff-puffs couldn't ever keep me awake.

The familiar but always beautiful view of the Bay of Naples dominated by smoking Vesuvius.

Li Galli, the Sirens' islands, three miles off the Italian coast just south of the Bay of Naples. Though Ulysses escaped the Sirens' charms with difficulty, the author climbed right up to their throne and joined their glee club.

The treacherous currents surging about the Sirens' islands have always made them dangerous to shipping. Even to-day any small boat caught in this cluster of jagged rocks runs a great risk of being destroyed.

Of course the path was easy enough to find and to follow, despite the darkness. I was exaggerating its elusiveness on purpose. We slid down-hill in a cloud of ash-dust and found our motor-car with nothing missing but the spare tire, the silver-figure radiator cup and ten gallons of gasoline.

# SIREN ISLES

# CHAPTER XVI

## SIREN ISLES

THE Bay of Naples tossed in the October wind as only the Bay of Naples can. Our small steamer, bound for Sorrento and Capri, alternated between nose-dives and tail-spins in the most seasickening manner. Jimmy and I regretted, as our deck chairs slid about among the prostrate passengers, that we had chosen to seek Sorrento by water instead of by motor. It was really the only thing to do, however. We had no idea how long we would be gone, or what we were going for, except that we were looking for Sirens; and on such a dangerous expedition we felt it best to be rid of such useless impedimenta as Mrs. Rolls-Royce.

We had two destinations in mind: the little Galli islands off the south coast of the Sorrento Peninsula, and the Blue Grotto at Capri. Legend insists the Sirens sang their fatal songs from the cliffs of Li Galli, but any one who has seen the Blue Grotto will champion its claims to the honor.

257

The nearest coastal town to Li Galli, where we
might hope to find a boat, was Positano on the Amalfi
road, eight miles from Sorrento.  Having planned
for a heavy schedule that day, to save time we took a
motor to cover this distance.  Reaching the summit of
an intervening ridge we could see the blue Gulf of
Naples dominated by Vesuvius glittering in the sun
on one side, and the just-as-blue Gulf of Salerno
spread itself out for our admiration on the other.
And there, in the latter bay, two miles out, apparently
barren of any vegetation or habitation, we first saw
the black bleak rocks past which Ulysses sailed,
struggling to break the ropes that prevented his
answering the Sirens' call.

On the beach at Positano, we found a number of
large row-boats drawn well up on the sand, for the
heavy wind, after two days' duration, was driving
tremendous breakers against the shore.  It was Sunday morning, and many of the fisherman were idling
at the café which faced the harbor.

Between Jimmy's Italian and my own, we explained that we wanted to be rowed out to Li Galli.
Our request was met with smiles and shoulder-
shrugs:—the weather was too rough—the waves
would capsize our boat before we could get it
launched—it would be very dangerous for the lady—
perhaps to-morrow or the next day the wind would
subside and allow us to go in safety.

One look at the roaring breakers was sufficient to convince us that they were right. We remembered what these same waves had done to our steamer crossing the Bay. I was all ready to abandon the idea and come back later. But not Jimmy.

"Oh nonsense!" she exclaimed. "I want to go now. I shouldn't care if we did turn over; can't imagine anything more agreeable than a swim after that dusty ride over the ridge. This weather isn't likely to subside for days. If we don't go now we never shall. Maybe if we offer them a hundred lire they won't think the trip quite so dangerous."

It was worth trying anyway.

"Will you go for one hundred lire?" I asked one of the boat owners.

"No, Signore."

"One hundred fifty?"

"No, Signore. It is too rough."

"Two hundred?" That was about ten dollars and well worth getting drowned for.

"*Si*, Signore. I'll go."

This did not settle the matter. We had to recruit three other men to help row, a rower for each of the four oars. It was only after I had offered a fifty-lire gratuity as a prize that we could get volunteers from the large crowd that had gathered around to watch the strange foreign couple perform.

Ten obliging friends of our crew pushed the boat

over the skids toward the water. Jimmy and 1
climbed aboard as a great breaker came roaring in.
Our man-power jumped after us just as the wave
ebbed, and the accommodating launchers, in water up
to their knees, with a shout gave the boat an heroic
shove.

Ulysses' rowers never fought harder to get clear
of the rock-hurling Cyclops than ours to get clear of
the Positano beach. Ulysses escaped; we didn't. The
succeeding wave caught us too quickly, lifted us like
a chip and flung us sideways back at the land, throw-
ing all six of us into a scrambled mass in the bottom of
the boat and burying everything under a roaring
mountain of cold water. A flying nine-foot oar gave
me a blow on the head. I saw a thousand stars. It
all happened in a flash. Jimmy! Where was Jimmy?
There she was struggling to her feet with half the
Gulf of Salerno streaming from her tailored coat-
suit, but still clinging to her gold vanity case and trying to laugh.

Never have I been so indignant at the ocean. My
enthusiasm for the Galli Islands had been only half-
hearted before. Now, by all the gods, I'd get there
if I had to swim! The four boatmen, gasping from
shock and cold water, gasped yet more when, the dory
having been dragged away from the lashing waves, I
got back in and ordered another attempt. The half-
drowned boat owner and I had a heated argument.

He wouldn't go back in that surf for *twice* two hun-dred lire.

His resistance only aroused my stubbornness the more. I had six hundred lire in cash with me, and I was willing to expend every centime of it, for I was *going to Li Galli!*

Still in my water-logged clothes I stood up in the dripping boat, waved equally wet bank-notes in the air at the crowd that had drawn close to enjoy all the details of this unexpected Sunday entertainment, and offered them to the three men who would risk another launching;—I'd take the fourth oar myself.

Ten dollars apiece! The temptation was too much. Three lads about seventeen accepted my bribe. Changing to another boat, we started the embarkation all over.

Jimmy begged to go again, and had she possessed a dry outfit,—why not?—since she swam like a fish. But a dry outfit she did not have. It would have been worse than foolhardy for her to sit two or three hours in her sodden clothes, in an open boat and in the October wind. She finally realized that herself and, deeply disappointed, agreed to accept the shelter of a hospitable matron's home until I returned.

Then the four of us got ready for a possible second drenching. We took off our shoes and coats and shirts and left them behind. One of the boys, named Giovanni, took a harmonica out of his trousers pocket and was about to place it for safe-keeping with his coat, when I asked him to bring the mouth organ along in case the Sirens wanted us to join their glee club.

A second time, standing up to our oars, we were pushed out with an ebbing wave, and this time by fast rowing and good luck, we got away. There was a loud cheer from the crowd on the beach. Jimmy, whose light blonde hair always made her distinguishable, waved bon voyage with her wet red felt hat.

Now that we were safe in the open sea, we decided to enjoy our little adventure. My companions were bright-faced, merry lads, greatly elated, despite the continued shower-bath we were getting from the flying spray, over the prospect of soon possessing so much money. Two hundred lire apiece! They'd go to Naples that very night and paint the town. Giovanni was so happy over the idea he began to sing *Funiculi, Funicula,* fortissimo, and the others joined in. While I didn't know the words, I knew the music and could tra-la-la as loud as they.

Tossing and plunging we skirted the coast, a sheer thousand-foot precipice, for three miles (Li Galli are not opposite Positano but three miles up the coast and two miles out), keeping about two hundred yards offshore, safely out of reach of the great rollers that raged against the adamantine cliffs. Reaching the point directly facing Li Galli we turned our boat and

*Funiculi-Funiculaed* straight for the seat of the Sirens.

Though the wind bore down with fresh fury, away from the shore, we stubbornly held our course with long, slow, steady strokes, until we came within the shadow of these inhospitable isles. There are three of them in a triangle; two are just great chimneys of rock, and the third, while quite as rocky, is sufficiently level in spots to permit a little vegetation. These three islets are scarcely a hundred feet apart. The waves surge through the narrow straits and clash and boil and boom. How easy it was to see what havoc the Sirens with their magic voices could have brought about, once they lured mariners into this sinister triangle of rocks and their lashing snarling waters!

On the leeward side of the largest isle was a small cove extending some twenty feet into the cliff, with a convenient ledge at one side. I wanted to get ashore if possible, and here was the only hope. Catching an incoming roller we rode it with a crash into this little gap in the rocks, using the oars as fenders. At the psychological moment I made a leap for the ledge and gained it, as the boat was dragged back by the ebb. Waiting for the next roller, the boat again tumbled into the cove, and, as Giovanni leaped, tumbled out again to stand by, manned by the two remaining men till we came back.

The young Italian and I climbed up the steep rock bank and sought the top of the highest cliff we could find overlooking the bursting breakers. Here surely the Sirens sat and sang. It was disappointing to find them departed after all our trouble. We wanted to join them in a music fest. Oh well, if we couldn't sing with them, we could sing without them. So we sat down on their rocky throne, our bare wet legs swing-ing over the edge, and while Giovanni accompanied me with irresistible allure on his harmonica, I sang *Funiculi, Funicula* at the top of my lungs.

We might have continued to improve on the Sirens for hours, had we not feared that the hypnotic call of our music might enchant the other two rowers and cause them to wreck our boat and drown, which would prevent our getting back to Positano for supper.

We had a hard enough time getting back as it was. But my guardian devil was on hand to see that Giovanni and I leaped and landed in our craft as it rode a breaker into the cove, and to see that it didn't capsize even when another roller lifted us high on the Positano beach.

Jimmy was awaiting our return, quite dry, neatly dressed, chic as ever, with her impudent nose gener-ously powdered, and her bobbed blonde hair blowing in the wind.

"You stayed so long I was afraid the Sirens had you," was her greeting.

"They almost did," I replied. "Especially the red-headed one. She had the most beautiful freckles,—just like yours, Jimmy. Only one thing saved us: Giovanni's harmonica. Just when all was lost, he played *Funiculi, Funicula* so ravishingly, the Sirens dropped their lyres to listen. That broke the spell and we rowed away like mad. They were awfully put out. Have you got my shirt? I'm dripping wet."

Jimmy had already telephoned to Sorrento for a motor to come after us. It was a touring car, and as there was plenty of room we waited till my well-paid young rowers had arrayed themselves in their Sunday clothes, and gave them a ride to Sorrento where they could take the boat to Naples and squander their two hundred lire in riotous living.

Early that afternoon Jimmy and I crossed to Capri, for while all the guide-books insisted that the Sirens had lived at Li Galli, I had not found a trace of them, and thought that the Blue Grotto might offer evidence of their having lived here.

Our very good intentions to visit the celebrated cave at once were doomed to disappointment. The stormy weather showed no signs of abatement as the day advanced, and we found, soon after landing, that only in calm seas was the low, tortuous grotto-entrance accessible.

Jimmy was loath to remain at Capri over night

since she had planned to be absent from her hotel in Naples for the day only, and had come away—as had I—without even so much as a tooth-brush. But I was equally loath to leave without a visit to the grotto, for it was unlikely we would have a chance to come again.

While we were arguing the matter the last boat that afternoon back to the mainland took advantage of our diverted attention and sneaked off without us. Now we *had* to stay.

Embarrassed by her lack of baggage, Jimmy refused to register at a hotel. A cab man came to our rescue and directed us to a small family pension where the proprietress, sympathizing with my companion's predicament, took her in and provided her, as she had been provided once before that day, with every requirement.

Jimmy was exceedingly impatient with me for having allowed the last boat to escape. Her surf-bathed costume, despite the application of hot irons at Positano, was still far from comfortable, so that the prospect of being away from her wardrobe another twenty-four hours was anything but an agreeable one. In a somewhat angry mood she even accused me—more justly that she guessed—of missing the boat on purpose, and to punish me maintained an icy aloofness as we sought the pension.

But her lodging turned out to be so snug and so

picturesque, and our dinner that night in a garden beneath the stars was so excellent, she forgave me my sins sufficiently to say good night with the old twinkle in her eyes, when, utterly weary from the day's adventures, I departed for my own hotel.

Although another entire day passed before the waves subsided, Jimmy became resigned to the delay, and managed, by supplementary purchases at the local shops plus continual encouragement from me, to maintain herself at the pension. A modern girl no longer needs a maid and seven trunks to keep presentable. With only one small piece of laundry soap, a basin of water, a fragile handkerchief and her vanity case, Jimmy worked miracles on her appearance. No girl in Capri was fresher-looking or better groomed than Jimmy.

The delay, unwelcome as it was, gave us a chance to prowl about the island, up this mountain and down that, never tiring of the dramatic pictures seen from the high places: Vesuvius to the north, Li Galli to the south, sea and sky and autumn air all about us; mountains and islands, colorful villas and terraced vineyards. Ulysses, though he may have passed right by the Blue Grotto on his way south from Circe's island to Sicily, did not land at Capri. It's just as well, for if he had he never *would* have got home.

Next day the wind and the thrashing waves died down. and scouts reported that access to the Blue

Grotto was possible. Renting one of the frail little grotto skiffs at Marina Grande, the port of Capri, Jimmy and I embarked once more to look for Sirens. Our equipment consisted of one lunch box, two bathing suits and a Turkish towel.

Modestly supplied with all the swimming requirements we bounced along the mile and half of beautiful precipitous coast to the obscure crack in the rocks that leads to the far-famed "Grotta Azzurra." We had chosen the noon hour for our expedition. The morning boatload of tourists from Naples had come and gone; the swarms of skiffs that conducted them into the sea-cave had disbanded, and there wouldn't be another deluge of tourists till afternoon. We should have the Blue Grotto all to ourselves. As I rowed toward the entrance I thought it best to enlighten my un-geological companion in regard to its history.

"Jimmy, if you'll stop telling me how to row this boat, I'll tell you some things you ought to know about our grotto."

"I don't trust you, Dick, after the information you gave me about art at the Naples Museum. You'll probably say the grotto was once a stable for sea-horses, or that a baptism in its waters will cure delirium tremens—and freckles."

"No, Jimmy," I said, deeply hurt. "I'll tell you only the gospel truth. I read it in a book while you were out buying bathing suits."

"All right, but don't you wander."

"Well, the book said that up till 1826—you weren't even born then—the cave had a very uncanny reputation. Fearful legends hung about it. It was said to be haunted by evil spirits, and nobody dared go inside. Every islander rowed rapidly past the opening in the cliff—tell me when we get there—half expecting to see some terrible monster come forth. One day a fisherman saw what he thought was a big fish swimming out of the cave. He threw his harpoon and struck it. Instead of a fish a bleeding man rose to the surface, shook his fist——"

"Now, Dickie——"

"But it's true, Jimmy. It's in the book. The fisherman fainted, was washed ashore in his boat and died in a week. And that isn't all. The book says some of the Capri fishermen still insist that every night after the German and American sight-seers have all gone home to bed, the Sirens sing sweetly there. So you see I wasn't wrong about the Sirens. They did and do live in this cave.

"Two German painters finally dared to investigate the dreadful place, and they found—oh well, what they found we'll find, because there's the entrance."

Through a narrow cleft in the cliff only three feet high where the water from the sea flows in and out, one must seek the cavern. The cleft isn't even high

enough to permit one to sit upright. Waiting for
an inrushing wave I seized the cable strung along the
tunnel and, lying flat in the boat to keep from bump-
ing my head, gave it a jerk which propelled us
through the keyhole.

We sat up and looked about—and caught our
breath, for we found ourselves floating no longer on
water, but on sky—iridescent, diaphanous, azure sky,
shot with blue-burning fire. Blue-blue-blue, silvery,
shimmering, fairy blue danced upon the walls, electri-
fied the quivering lake of jewels, turned the stalactite
ceiling to great soft sapphires and touched the very
air with supernatural spirits, overwhelming us with
its radiant, magical, glorious, blue beauty.

"Dick! We've died and gone to Heaven."
Jimmy at last found words to speak.

But it wasn't Heaven. It was real,—a caprice of
nature such as the fairies with all their witchery could
never have created. Some literal scientist has come
along and analyzed its loveliness, explained its harmony, dissected its enchantment. He tells us the
Blue Grotto is not the Spirit of Beauty imprisoned
in a cave, but the result of sunshine entering through
a submerged window in the sea-wall of the cavern,
which causes the white light to be refracted, absorb-
ing all the color rays except the blue which is allowed
to penetrate the interior and tinge everything with
its own pure, translucent hue. Close the submerged

window, and you have only a dark hole in the rocks, where the Sirens, deprived of their eerie illumination, would no longer have the heart to sing.

One of the amazing features of the Grotto is the magic effect its water has on anything dipped beneath it. An oar, a hand, is turned to flaming silver, leaving ripples of fire in its wake. We had come to swim in this phantom blue, and we must hasten while the Grotto was all our own.

"Dick, we didn't bring along a bath-house. Where am I going to undress?"

"Oh, use the boat. I'll close my eyes, count sheep and whistle."

"No sir! I won't change in this sea-shell. It's too rockety. I want to preserve my coat-suit from any more salt-water bathing. It's still in very poor health after Positano."

"Then we can use Tiberius' landing-place there on the side. It leads to a gallery fifty yards deep that once connected the cave with the emperor's villa above. I read that in the book too. You put your Mother-Hubbard on in the passage and I'll stand guard outside to keep the mermen away."

Jimmy disappeared into the gallery, saying something caustic about mer*maids*. When she reappeared presently, in a bathing suit, I was in mine, and together we dived into the cold, bottomless, blue incandescence. Ten million burning bubbles rose to

the surface.  We were transformed to great silvery
fish that stirred the sapphire sky we swam upon with
sapphire flames.  Remembering my quest for sponges
at lotus land, I pushed my way deep down and, opening my eyes, found myself in a glassy sea of limpid
azure light.  It was not water; it was light, light, we
drifted in.

As I watched, Jimmy dived from the ledge and
plunging downward became a fiery comet with a
nebulous tail of sparks.  The agitated water cast phosphorescent reflections all about us, and the whole
Grotto danced and glittered.

Then I would dive and Jimmy watch.  Then
Jimmy was a porpoise and I a seal.  We splashed and
shouted and reveled in this airy fairy world.  Every
sound reverberated against the gleaming walls, and,
as reluctantly I put my earthly vest and pantaloons
back on, I made the celestial grotto ring with the
magnificent strains of *Funiculi, Funicula.*

That evening, while all Capri was asleep, Jimmy
and I tramped across the island, following the trail
that led at length to the ruins of the Roman villa
directly over the cavern we had swum in that noon.
Steep rock-hewn steps led down the cliff-face to the
grotto's entrance.  Not a soul was near.  Even the
wind had deserted this haunted spot, and only the
subdued waves broke the stillness.

As we looked with dreamy eyes out over the starlit

ocean, from within the cavern faint music came to us softly through the darkness. Prosaic people would have said it was the sound of water lapping on the grotto walls. But we knew that was not true. We knew it was the sweet soft voices of Ulysses' Sirens—singing.

# BETWEEN SCYLLA AND CHARYBDIS

# CHAPTER XVII

## BETWEEN SCYLLA AND CHARYBDIS

BACK in Naples we found Mignon, Jimmy's equally English traveling companion, in a state of great excitement. She had returned from Rome unexpectedly to find Jimmy gone and to learn from the hotel clerks that her friend had departed several days before with "the American." Mignon had never heard of "the American,"—certainly no one that Jimmy might do the disappearing act with. The motor-car was still safe in the garage, so evidently she had not "eloped with the chauffeur." That was some consolation.

In preparation for our reception—if we ever *did* come back—Mignon had prepared a long moral lecture full of big words she was going to deliver to her wayward comrade, but when the bubbling, breezy, unrepentant Jimmy came bursting into their hotel, Mignon saw the hopelessness of trying to reform such an irrepressibly happy soul and, instead, listened with honest envy to the enthralling description of our crimes.

277

Mignon was a perfect complement to Jimmy.
With her dark eyes and hair she was handsomer than
Jimmy but not so gay. She was an angel; Jimmy an
imp. There was an air of dignity about her. No one
ever called her "Min"—till I did. I had to do something reckless to win her favor after having absconded
with the only companion she had,—and this worked.

That night the three of us dined sumptuously together and discussed the next act.

"Didn't Ulysses have some interesting adventure
with two nice girls, on his travels in this part of the
world?" Min asked.

"He probably didn't know any nice girls, if he
was anything like a lot of his Greek descendants I saw
in Athens," Jimmy interjected.

I flew to my hero's defense. "You're all wrong
there, Jimmy. Ulysses was always a gentleman. He
was gone from his wife *twenty years,* and in all that
time only two women ever broke down his fidelity to
Penelope—Circe and Calypso—and they were both
goddesses, so he couldn't help it. Ulysses' character
was entirely *too* irreproachable.

"But we're off the subject. No, Min; unfor-
tunately, Ulysses didn't have any more adventures in
Italy after he left the Sirens behind, except with
Scylla,—and she was anything but a 'nice girl,' considering the way she ate six of Ulysses' men for
breakfast without even cooking them."

"Oh, that reminds me," exclaimed Jimmy. "You never did finish telling me what happened to Ulysses when he passed between Scylla and Charybdis. You were just about to, on top Vesuvius, when you grew tired of talking and wanted to hold hands. Remember?"

"Yes, I remember. Well it's a sad story. Ulysses sailed on down the west coast with a heavy heart. He didn't dare tell his men what terrors lay ahead of them for fear they'd refuse to go on. That is, he didn't tell them about Scylla. There was no keeping Charybdis a secret. As they approached the narrow straits they saw a cloud of vapor and heard a mighty roar and dropped their oars in terror. Ulysses pleaded with them to take courage. Of course he knew there was really no hope for some of them, for any moment Scylla might seize the very men he was trying to encourage. But though he lost twice six of his comrades, they must keep as far away as possible from the sucking, roaring whirlpool on the other side. So he ordered his helmsman to steer the ship close beneath Scylla's rock. Then arming himself he stood at the prow anxiously waiting for whatever might happen.

"Closer and closer they came to the hungry Charybdis. The maelstrom was sucking in the water with a dreadful noise, and with eddies so deep one could see the sand on the bottom. Every one, with his heart in his mouth, gazed in terror at the whirlpool, expecting each moment to be his last,—when swoop!— Scylla with a hideous cry suddenly reached her six long arms out of her cave and snatched up six of Ulysses' men. Writhing in their death struggles and screaming for their leader, they were lifted high into the cave and devoured gluttonously by the savage Scylla. In after days Ulysses said this was the most sickening sight he saw throughout all his voyages.

"Fortunately, at this heavy price, they escaped Charybdis, and getting through the straits, sailed safely on down the Sicilian coast to anchor at the harbor of Taormina."

"Not Taormina!" Min exclaimed. "Why that's the place we've been intending to go for weeks. I hear it's the most beautiful town in Sicily. Everybody I've ever seen who has been there simply raves about it. It seems the town has Mount Ætna for a background and the ocean for a foreground and is filled with flowers and artists and invalids and Englishmen. Of course you're going if Ulysses did."

"Certainly I am—I must. I've got to go to Messina first though, and see if Scylla is as bad as Homer paints her. I understand the Charybdis whirlpools are still there—actually."

"When are you going, Dickie?" Jimmy asked. I tried to detect some note of alarm in her inquiry, but I couldn't.

"Pretty soon now. I want to swim the straits.
I've wanted to ever since I got across the Hellespont.
Wouldn't it be great sport to swim from Scylla to
Charybdis? I'm told it's never been done,—probably
because nobody ever thought of it but me. I must
hurry, because to-morrow is the twenty-seventh of
October. The water's getting awfully cold. Don't
you remember how cold it was in the Blue Grotto?"

"Why not let's all go?" suggested Min. "The only
reason Jimmy and I have hesitated this long is because it means taking the Rolls-Royce so far from
a service station. We'll feel safer if you're along.
You can fix punctures and wiggle things when the
engine goes dead."

"All right. But remember, lady, I'm a union
man, and if you don't like the way I wiggle things,
don't you try to hire anybody else. I'll have my
rights."

Fortified with their pledge to observe union
rules—whatever they were—I secured road maps
next morning, and by afternoon Min and Jimmy and
I, all on the front seat, our baggage in the rear, were
whirling southward,—through Resina (with a new
spare tire and radiator cap), past Sorrento, and over
the familiar road to Positano. Li Galli had not moved
since Giovanni and I had concertized upon the Sirens'
throne. We tarried at Positano to say hello to our
young mouth-organist friend and inquire about his

riotous excursion to Naples, but found that, although
a week had elapsed since his departure, he was still
rioting.

We stopped for the night at the famous Capuchin
Monastery high up above the harbor of Amalfi, and
next day, having visited the stately Greek temples at
Pæstum, sped on down the coast some hundred and
fifty miles more. The next afternoon despite twisting
mountain roads we approached the Straits of Messina.

About five miles before reaching the ferry-boat,
we came to the picturesque little town of Scilla
(modern Italian spelling), built partly on a high
naked promontory of rock that thrusts itself boldly
into the sea. This great rock was the home of the
voracious Scylla. There is a local legend that up to
the eighteenth century a cavern opened upon the sea,
but that repeated earthquakes have destroyed all signs
of what was possibly Scylla's cave. Raising its shining head two hundred feet sheer from the water, and
dominating the entrance to the straits, Scylla could
not have chosen a more strategic watch-tower for
observing any ship that dared choose the Italian coast
in favor of the whirlpool of Sicily.

From the battlements of the medieval castle on
top the cliff, one clearly sees the extreme northeast
corner of Sicily. It was disappointing to find the
straits so wide here, for though the channel is only
two-and-one-half miles across from this point of Sicily

to the place directly opposite on the Italian shore, Scylla, located two miles higher up the coast, is four miles away from the point.

It took small imagination to look over the brink of this Rock and picture Ulysses' ship coasting fearfully along its base to avoid the roaring Charybdis; or to picture the consternation among the crew, when the six-armed monster fell like a thunderbolt upon them and horribly devoured six writhing Greeks before Ulysses' very eyes.

I was so intent on picturing the dreadful tragedy that I had no desire to climb down from my Scyllan clouds and return to earth. But Min and Jimmy could be such prosaic young women at times. They insisted that sitting on a hard rock one whole hour was enough for anybody, and pulled me back to the road. We raced to the ferry station, ran the motorcar on to a ferry-boat and crossed the fabulous straits to Sicily.

It was a sparkling, late October afternoon as the boat pushed away for Messina, and for me, a sparkling moment. Here was the channel famed in song and story,—notoriously treacherous and violent. Here Ulysses, reeling from the ghastly encounter with Scylla, five miles back, had sailed with his unhappy Greeks, fleeing into open water again, with the screams of his comrades and the bellowing of Charybdis still ringing in his ears. Except at Troy, and Ithaca itself, I have never felt so close to Ulysses as in this channel. Never had he seemed so real, so tangible. Here was one great anchor of historic fact to which I could cling in trying to reconstruct his travels, for there is no possible doubt that the Straits of Messina flow between the Rock of Scylla and the Whirlpool of Charybdis.

In the city of Messina I deserted Min and Jimmy. While this place was all important to me, there was nothing of interest to hold them here. So I sped my friends on their way to Taormina, thirty miles farther down the coast. Jimmy insisted that if I were going to swim the channel she wanted to be alongside in a boat, but I knew that several days of preliminary reconnaissance would be necessary before the final attempt, and that even then I might abandon the idea. And so, though it would have been great fun to have her along, I insisted they go on ahead without me.

Immediately I began to investigate distances, currents, etc., and found that unless the whirlpool had changed its position since Homer's time, the poet had been slightly misinformed in regard to the topography of the straits, for Charybdis, instead of being directly opposite Scylla's Rock, lies eight miles to the south, just outside the sickle-like peninsula that protects the harbor of Messina.

From the top of the lighthouse that rises above the sickle, one enjoys a splendid view of the whirlpool only a hundred yards offshore. It is called in Italian *garofano* (carnation), for, with its rapidly curling choppy, white-topped waves, it resembles nothing so much as this flower. The whirling pool is a gigantic eddy caused by the powerful rush of the tides past the obstructing peninsula. With them it waxes and wanes. I looked down upon it at the height of its disturbance, eleven A. M., and realized that while a modern steamer would pass through it unharmed, a comparatively small sailboat such as Ulysses had would be completely helpless in its clutches.

This is by no means the only whirlpool. There are several others, much smaller and far less dangerous, farther up the channel, but it was in all probability upon sailors' tales of the *garofano* itself that Homer built his terrible Charybdis. While the smaller pools are not powerful enough to endanger even the fishing boats, they certainly can wreck a swimmer. I'll vouch for *that*.

If I had any secret hopes of actually plunging into Charybdis and swimming through it across to Scylla, eight miles away, they were quickly shattered after one glance at the tidal currents that gallop through this bottle-neck channel alternately back and forth every six hours. The Hellespont adventure had only proved to me that I was far from being a sea-lion—especially far in currents. Certainly I couldn't last out eight miles of such obstreperous wintry water.

The currents would land me under Jimmy's nose at the Taormina beach, or up at Stromboli, before I got across, depending on which way the tides were moving.

However, there were other *garofanos* and other possibilities. At the tip of Sicily, the straits, as I have said, are only two and one-half miles wide, and though Scylla is four miles away from the tip, this distance across to the Rock was less than my Hellespont swim. I believed that if I could catch the north rushing tide I might be able to gain Scylla, as I had gained Abydos, before the current carried me past. At least there was no harm in trying everything once. And if I failed, what of it? It would have been a fine gesture.

The trolley took me up the coast to the Point. Here there is another great lighthouse, and a small fishing village. Innumerable fishing boats were lined up along the beach, and I believed that I could hire one of them with rowers to accompany me across.

The moment I approached a boatman and made my request, the news spread that a crazy foreigner was going to swim to Scylla. Fifty people gathered round to inspect the curiosity and tell me that at this hour the tide was flowing furiously south—I'd be carried back to Messina—better come again to-morrow morning. I did, and this time the tide was flowing just as furiously north. I thought this would be ideal, but the fishermen insisted we'd all be swept out into the open sea. Better wait till noon when the currents were changing and comparatively quiet. Even then they insisted no one ever had swum from their village to Scylla, and no one ever would. Just look at the little whirlpools all along the shore, and the way the water was swirling now forward, now backward, now across, in a perfect bedlam of currents. And they swore the channel was infested with sharks which collected in the Messina vicinity to feed on the refuse. If I was determined to go I would have to wear a rope around my waist by which they could drag me in if need be.

Noon came, and the changing tides. The water seemed rougher than ever. In mid-stream the froth-ing white caps were dancing south; nearer land they were rushing north, and close to the shore the little *garofanos* were whirling stronger than ever. I looked across to the great beckoning Rock of Scylla with a sinking heart—so close, and yet so far.

There was none of the old Hellespont spirit surg-ing within, as I ordered the men to launch the boat. There was no Leander and no Lord Byron to have blasted a path. There was no bright burning sun-shine here, and no bright sapphire sea. The sky had that day become overcast; it was a November sky, glowering and dark. The straits looked cold and gray. There was no faithful Roderic to encourage me. (Why, oh why, had I let Jimmy go?) There was no precedent, no life-long dream, no romantic inspiration, to spur me on. I loved every wave in the poetic old Hellespont; but these ominous swirls and whirlpools reminded me of angry snakes. I entered the Hellespont with a song in my heart; I entered the Straits of Messina with clenched teeth and grim determination.

The entire village lined up on the shore to see us off. I disappointed two hundred people by not putting on a red bathing suit and plunging dramatically into the largest whirlpool. If I had, that would have been just as far as I should have got. It was necessary to proceed beyond the *garofanos* strung along the shore, if I hoped to have any life left in me for the remaining four miles. So I climbed in the boat and was rowed beyond them.

As at Positano, a man stood up to each one of the four oars. We pushed away and fought across the intervening eddies to be driven a hundred yards along the shore before we were a hundred yards away from it. The whirlpools behind us, I stripped and was about to dive overboard when the boat-owner caught me by the arm and wanted to fasten the anti-shark rope about my waist. It was the anchor rope and half an inch thick. I stormed with impatience at such a preposterous idea—I'd rather be eaten by sharks than try to swim with such an impediment. He expostulated and gesticulated,—pantomiming the shark's terrific jaws clamping upon my leg and dragging me down if I didn't have the safeguard of the rope; and his pulling me nimbly alongside and giving the big fish a punch in the nose, if I did. I was *still* obdurate and once more was about to leap, when the fisherman became threatening and vowed that if I refused to use the rope, he'd refuse to accept the responsibility, row straight back to shore and abandon the whole enterprise.

With a mixture of rage and despair, I submitted to the harness, and, attached to the rowers by fifteen feet of tether, at last dived in.

God! What cold water! I came to the surface gasping from shock, and struck out furiously. Before I'd gone a hundred feet the hemp hawser was tangled up in my legs and dragging me down by its weight. I tried to sneak out of it in the water where that devil holding the other end couldn't see what I was doing till too late. The old fox's eyes, however, were too sharp for me. Before I had more than started to untie the knot, he began to haul me in to the accompaniment of more dire threats. *Why* wasn't Jimmy here! *She'd* have some sense. And to think it was I who had sent her on ahead. Fool!

I glanced back to shore, and the people standing there looked half a mile away already. This was only because we were being swept parallel to the shore so rapidly, and not because I'd swum any great distance from it. I must redouble my efforts if I intended to reach Scylla before I froze to death.

Longer, slower strokes began to get me somewhere, though the ten-ton cable reduced my efficiency by at least a third. In about half an hour I had crossed the north-bound current and reached the south-bound, having been spun about and battledored and shuttlecocked by the whirlpools at the dividing line.

Just as I had been driven north for over half a mile, I now began to sail southward. In half an hour more I found myself back in line with the fishing station, and no more than a mile out. One mile nearer Scylla in one hour! And I was already getting numb. The Hellespont cold was hellfire and brimstone compared to this. The rope swelled and was tightening around my waist. The hatred I expended on the rope exhausted me much more than the swim.

The mid-channel south-bound current seemed endlessly broad. Every time I looked toward Scylla it was farther north. In another half-hour I was beginning to despair of ever getting there when an especially entangling alliance with the hemp boa constrictor broke the last straw of my resolution. I had the boatmen drag me in and remove the hated shackles. I acknowledged myself hopelessly beaten. But as no one else, so far as I can ascertain, has ever swum the straits either, I need not have felt so bad about it.

We were now half-way across the channel and one-third the way to Scylla. If I couldn't swim the rest of the distance, I'd sail it; so I ordered the boatmen to raise their canvas and get me to Italy.

To my surprise they refused—they must return to Sicily—I was so slow a swimmer the tide had changed and all the water in the channel would soon be sweeping south—they might not be able to get back for six hours—it would be night then. No, by all the saints they weren't going another foot toward Italy.

This was all that was necessary to bring to a climax my smoldering anger against the boatmen and the rope and the water and the currents and the world in general. I vowed by all the saints they *were* going. No Scylla—no lire! They understood that all right, and stopped to reconsider, since it was a fat rate I had offered them for their services,—at least five times what a native would have paid. With a sly leer they agreed to complete the crossing if I'd double their promised reward. Such banditry added fuel to my flames of indignation. Even then I was so determined to land upon Scylla's Rock I would have submitted to the pirates had I had the extra money. I didn't have it; I had left my surplus funds behind in Messina, in the hotel-safe, bringing along only the amount of lire I thought I'd need.

Money or no money, I was not going to permit
their unscrupulousness to wreck an idea I had pursued for three days and already wasted so much time
on.  I pretended to subside, and agreed to meet their
demands.  Satisfied, and smiling at my gullibility,
they raised the sail and presently beached on the sand
below the Rock.  Here I gave them the overlarge fee
agreed upon in Sicily, and no more.  It was all I had
except five lire for transportation to Messina.

One could have heard their howls in Naples, and it
was music to my ears.  I made them a low and sweeping bow and strode off toward the town.

But that by no means ended it.  They were right
at my heels, and had it been dark enough, would have
given me a good murdering for my remaining five
lire.

A gendarme, hearing the boatmen's groans of
agony, came up.  On being told the story of my de-
fault, he arrested me and conducted us all to the
tumble-down police station.  The Chief was not on
hand.  To his assistant the four scoundrelly fishermen vowed I had refused to pay them more than half
the guaranteed fee, which they swore was one-fifth the
amount I had actually put into their hands.  The
police lieutenant, with sufficient pantomime for me to
understand, ordered me to meet my obligations or be
locked up till the Chief returned to-morrow.  I refused.  I didn't have the amount of "my obligations,"

and if I had had, even though the situation was
becoming unendurably humiliating, I should still have
refused.

The police then searched me and found only the
five lire. I didn't have even a passport. It too had
been left in Messina. I had nothing but my cold
word that I had filled the agreement made in Sicily
and paid *ten times* over the amount the boatmen had
acknowledged receiving. In the face of their hysteri-
cal denials my word was naturally discredited.

Seeing that I really had no more money, my
persecutors dropped their demands, and insisting
they must get back across the channel "before the tide
got too strong," were dismissed.

The lieutenant by no means dismissed *me*. My
supposed refusal to understand his Italian, my lack
of passport and money, my utterly demented attempt
to swim the straits, my absurd knee-length knicker-
bockers, and this deliberate, criminal acceptance of a
service from poor, simple, downtrodden peasants, for
which I knew I could not pay, all stamped me as a
suspicious and dangerous rogue. In fact I was probably a spy. To jail with me!

I spent the night locked up in an empty anteroom
of the police station. For supper the lieutenant gave
me a glass of water and a dish of cold, pasty spaghetti,
which, ravenous as I was from the long frigid battle
with the straits, I could not swallow. The rage and

humiliation that had been boiling hotter and hotter all afternoon must have scorched the miserable cot I had to lie on, thinking up diabolic tortures for the police lieutenant. Undoubtedly he was one of Scylla's own brood.

The night dragged itself sleeplessly, sullenly, along. It wasn't the shame of imprisonment I minded so much. I'd been in before,—at Gibraltar. There, however, I had an honest trial for the honest crime of taking forbidden photographs. There the whole thing was a romantic adventure, a real genuine drama, shot full of good humor, and handled with dignity and courtesy by army majors and English judges.

But this was only despicableness and discomfort. How had I ever allowed myself to sink into such an ignoble predicament? I wondered if I'd tell Jimmy, and if I did tell her, what she'd say,—most likely laugh for ten minutes. Jimmy found humor in every-thing. She'd probably think the cold spaghetti *especially* funny.

Next morning I was marched before the Chief. I told him, with the assistance of a townsman who had been to America and spoke a little English, that if he'd telephone my hotel in Messina, the manager who had my passport and check-book would verify my story. This he had the extraordinarily good sense to do, and though he still felt sure, along with his assistant, that any one who wore such funny pants as mine and tried to swim the straits in November, was a sinister character, he gave me back my five lire and reluctantly set me free—without any breakfast.

Five lire! Five miles to the ferry! Should I purchase food and walk or go hungry and ride? I went hungry—as far as the first restaurant that served fruit and eggs and chocolate.

Thus fortified against any further outrages, I started to walk along the same highway Min and Jimmy and I had motored over in our million-dollar Rolls-Royce four days previously. Reaching a point on the coast elevated well above the straits where the road turns a sharp corner and shuts the scene of all this action from view, I looked back and made faces at the city of Scylla and its damned Rock. Then asking Heaven with every step to bless the good kind Italians, I tramped majestically on through the dust.

# CITY OF THE SUN GOD

# CHAPTER XVIII

## CITY OF THE SUN GOD

THAT afternoon at the crowded Taormina railroad station I looked about anxiously for Jimmy's bright red hat. I had wired her in advance of my arrival, and believed she would meet me. But there was not a red hat to be seen! My disappointment was painful. I had missed her so keenly—and she evidently didn't care whether I came or not. I stood on the platform as the other passengers moved away, feeling, and probably looking, thoroughly glum. I had thought——

"Dick!"

I whirled about. It was Jimmy's voice. It was *Jimmy*. She had been standing near by all the time and I hadn't recognized her. And no wonder! She wasn't wearing her red sport hat; she wasn't wearing her leather motor coat or the well-known blue coat-suit; she wasn't even wearing her brogue shoes. Instead, a floppy black hat hid her merry eyes, and a smart black dress, that I had not seen before, completed the disguise.

"You look as if you had just found a hole in your
new red-top boots," she laughed as I leaped joyfully
to greet her.

"I thought you hadn't come, Jimmy.  I was look-
ing everywhere for freckled noses and small red hats.
I never thought to look for you under a big black one.
Isn't it new?—and the *swell* black dress?"

"Why, Dick! you *noticed* it!  I never even hoped
you would.  Your wire came this noon, and I
hated to meet you in the old red ruin.  So I made
Mignon give me this one.  She bought it in Rome,
and was saving it until she met the king.  Why didn't
you come *much* sooner?"

"I came as soon as I could.  The police had me
till this morning."

"So that's where you've been!  I'm not surprised.
Mignon and I both knew you'd get into trouble the
moment we left."

"I know it, Jimmy.  I lost all of my luck soon
as you went away.  I tried to swim the cursed straits,
and the currents made fun of me, and there wasn't
any sun, and I almost froze to death, and my boatmen
made me wear a rope, and half-way across I began
to die and had to give up.  Then I had a squabble
with the boatmen, and I was arrested at Scylla and
put in the police station for all of last night, and made
to sleep on an awful cot, and fed cold clammy
spaghetti; and then I didn't have any money and had

to walk home. Oh, and a lot more! It's just what happens whenever you desert me,—I can't even keep out of jail!"

"*Me desert you!*" she exclaimed. "You know I wanted to stay and go along in the rowboat. You wouldn't even *listen* to me."

"I know it. I'll listen next time."

"But I'm sorry you failed to swim across. You seemed to want to so badly. I'll tell you what!" she said with sudden inspiration. "Let's go back and try it again."

I almost collapsed.

Jimmy had not brought the motor-car to meet me. The town of Taormina lies six hundred feet above the harbor and station, and the communicating road is such a steep tortuous one that a cab is the best means of traveling it.

At the hotel we had a gay reunion with Min and, as it was time for tea, had it served on the hotel balcony overlooking the sea and the rose garden. There they told me about their safe, escortless journey from Messina, and I gave them all the gory details of my encounter with Scylla and Charybdis.

We didn't drink much tea. It got cold while we watched the sun set against the snow-clad summit of Mount Ætna.

This glorious volcano dominates Taormina with majestic tyranny. It is a graceful, sky-scraping background for every landscape. It blocks the vista down each ancient street. One sees it through the almond trees; one watches it glow and fade as the seasons and the sunlight paint its slopes; one greets it each morning when one wakes, and looking out the window sees this queenly mountain rising from the sea almost eleven thousand feet, framed in the purple clematis that climbs about one's balcony.

For two magic weeks Min and Jimmy and I clung to Taormina. We climbed up the venerable villages perched dramatically on neighboring mountain-tops; we met all the "artists and invalids and Englishmen." Though it was November in the unhappy world without, in the hotel gardens here the walls were covered with roses, and the orange trees bent low with their bright fruit.

If I felt that I should look about for some good excuse to defend this long relaxation from my pursuit of Ulysses, I was not long finding it in the fact that Ulysses tarried here himself for a month or more. True, our reasons for delaying the journey on to Ithaca were not the same. Ulysses' departure was held up by contrary winds; mine, by the hypnotic charm of Taormina's sky and sea and flowers and colorful society, and by the lure of Min's and Jimmy's comradeship.

Enchanting as it was, Ulysses did not wish to land at Taormina for the Sun God's cattle grazed here, and Teiresias, in Hades, had warned him that, should his followers even by chance harm one, it would bring about the destruction of the ship and its crew. So he instructed the rowers to head away from such a dangerous place.

But for once Ulysses' wishes were not followed by his men. They had rowed four hundred miles from Monte Circeo and now demanded that they be given a rest on shore.

Fearful of this move, but unable to oppose his entire company, he granted their request, and exhorting them not to touch the cattle, beached the ship. Their landing place was undoubtedly in the harbor of what is now Taormina, for here the first break in the long straight shore-line south of Charybdis offers a refuge for ships.

That night the Greeks slept on the sand and, because of contrary winds, for the thirty nights that followed. Their provisions supplied by Circe became exhausted. Hunger began to press them seriously. Even Ulysses was forced to forage as best he could for food.

One day during his absence the Greeks became desperate and, deciding they would rather die instantly from the Sun God's wrath than by inches from starvation, slaughtered several of the inviolate cattle.

Furious at this sacrilege, the Sun God sought

Jupiter on Mount Olympus and threatened to cease shining unless the father of the gods punished the guilty Greeks. Punishment was promised,—quick, deadly punishment; and so Helios went back into the firmament, content.

Yet for six days the doomed Greeks feasted on. The seventh day, the wind changed to the west, and they set sail once more, toward Ithaca. It was to be their last voyage.

From the Greek Theater, built into the end of a high promontory that overshadows the harbor, one can look down and see the probable beach from which Ulysses' ship sailed away to meet the judgment of Jupiter.

The panorama from the rim of this theater, with the ancient castles perched high above, the mountains of Italy across the narrowing straits, and the vision of glittering Ætna soaring gracefully out of the boundless blue, is truly one of the great sights of Sicily. No day was ever complete for Jimmy and Min and me, regardless of how filled with color and happy adventure it may have been, until we climbed from the orchestra to the topmost gallery of this theater and felt our spirits soar within us as we looked back beyond the ancient stage, across the ocean and the purple valleys, to the great white poem in the clouds.

One morning when the early sun was tinging

Ætna's snows with rainbow lights, Mignon put into words a feeling about the mountain that Jimmy and I likewise felt.

"Ætna doesn't seem like other mountains to me. It's more like a human being that has a great magnetic personality. I can't keep my eyes off it. It's the last thing I look for at night, and the first thing in the morning. I can just sit and stare at it all day."

"I feel the same way, Min," I said. "I feel myself being pulled toward it. I wonder if anybody ever climbs the old thing?"

"Of course they do," exclaimed Jimmy. "I'll climb it if you will; and you, Mignon, even though Ulysses didn't do it. We three would have a great time."

"But, my children," warned the more cautious Min, "it's almost the middle of November. It will be frightfully cold on top."

"Good!" said Jimmy. "I've wanted to be an Eskimo ever since I can remember. Here's my chance."

"Me too," I agreed. "If you two mountain goats will get the motor out I'll have the hotel fix us a basket of blubber, or walrus oil, or whatever it is Eskimos live on."

In an hour we were off for Mount Ætna, supplied with what proper clothes and heavy shoes we could scrape together. Our climbing equipment consisted

mostly of a huge lunch basket, six pint bottles of
champagne, and an Alice-blue Rolls-Royce. The
hotel manager told us to go to Nicolosi, about forty
miles away and well up the slope of the mountain
facing the sea. The road that far was good. We
could get guides there to conduct us to the summit,
twelve miles beyond.

We reached Nicolosi without mishap and engaged
an experienced guide. He tried to discourage us:
the summit was already deep in snow; the winds blew
violently; it would be exceedingly cold; we should
have woolen helmets; the observatory building near
the top where we would have to spend the night was
not suitable for ladies.

Jimmy's reply to all this was only to ask what
time we started.

"To-morrow morning at five o'clock if you are
determined to go, Signorina."

And at five, with one horse to carry the "blubber,"
we were in motion, walking upward, upward, through
the chestnut groves that grew luxuriantly in the deep
lava ash. The base of Ætna is ninety miles in circumference, and this entire great area at one time or
another has been flooded with lava, for Ætna, though
its eruptions are irregular, is one of the liveliest volcanoes in the world.

At eight thousand feet we struck the snow and the
wind. Already we regretted the silly impetuosity

with which we had tumbled into this climb. We were wearing the heaviest shoes we possessed, but the snow seeped through, and the cold wind bit to the very marrow.

There was no grumbling. Though Mignon was not so athletically inclined as Jimmy, she was just as cheerful a sport. We had danced into this mountain climb in a larking spirit, and we were determined that it was going to be a lark even if we froze to death and were buried on top. So we made light of our frosty feet, helped one another up the dangerous places and laughed at the increasingly savage opposition of the wind. A flask of brandy I had thoughtfully brought along helped make the laughing easier.

As we approached the observatory building at nine thousand seven hundred feet, where a room is reserved for climbers, Jimmy hesitated to enter.

"If I go near a fire now," she shouted above the young blizzard, "I'll thaw too quickly and spoil."

"Oh, it's only a handful of charcoals," I shouted back encouragingly. "You'll be safe."

We pushed through the door and closed it with a bang. Two tiers of broad bunks piled high with blankets almost filled the room. Antonio, our guide, got the pot of charcoal to burning. Min and Jimmy filled the kettle with snow and put it over the coals to make tea. I emptied my pockets of the chestnuts I had stuffed them with on the way up and, amid loud

praise from my companions for this noble idea, I set
them—along with our shoes—to roasting.

The crater rim was yet another thousand feet
above, and, realizing how ill-prepared we were to face
the summit blasts more than once, we decided to postpone the final dash till early next morning when we
could  watch the sun rise from the rim.

Through the fast gathering twilight Min and
Jimmy and Antonio and I, all wrapped in blankets,
huddled about the coals and dined on the "walrus oil"
and two of the bottles of champagne.  At eight
o'clock, Antonio ordered us to sleep,—an order which,
with blankets piled about us, and a twelve-mile climb
behind us, and ninety-seven hundred feet below us,
we found very easy to obey.

Long before sunup, our brutal conductor dragged
us out again.  With pieces of rope we each draped a
blanket about head and shoulders to serve as a top
coat.  Under this ethereal head-dress Min, with her
dark expressive eyes, made a perfect Madonna.
Jimmy said that at last my Eskimo dream had come
true,—I looked just like one.

Whirrrr!  The wind all but swept us off our feet
as we left the shelter of the building and braved the
elements again.  It was a clear night, for the full
moon, which had not yet set, shone upon our high
peak of snow like day.  Fighting every foot against
the freezing blast, we clung to our blankets with one

hand, and dug our walking sticks into the snow with
the other. There was no time to laugh now during
this last, steep, slick thousand feet. It demanded
care and every ounce of effort to keep the wind from
lashing us down the side of the iceberg. We were so
intent upon our climb we scarcely noticed that the
breaking dawn was giving us increasing light.

With one last effort we gained the rim and, feeling
that we were on the top of the world, peered over into
the terrifying abyss. It was a mass of whirling smoke
and steam and clouds driven savagely about by the
wind. The crater floor, eight hundred feet below,
was hidden, and the opposite walls, one-third of a
mile away, were only a blur. The gravel and ashes
and bits of ice and snow, that were fired at us from
out the great seething chasm, stung like needles. It
would have been suicide, with our insufficient clothing, to expose ourselves here more than a few brief
moments. It wasn't that we could not have stood
the cold had we been wearing enough sweaters and
mittens and helmets. I had been on top the Matterhorn in October and Fujiyama in January and stood
it well enough, but in neither case was I chiefly de-
pendent for protection, as here, on the warmth afforded by the bright blueness of my shirt and cravat
(which matched the shirt most elegantly) and a
blanket flapping hysterically about my ears.

We had not timed our final ascent accurately with

the sunrise, for we were back at the observatory before the first sparks began to fly over the east. Using
the small stone building as a windshield and resorting
to the brandy to lessen our rigors, we stood shiver-
ingly and watched one of the sublime pictures of the
world unfold.

Hovering close to earth an ocean of soft white
clouds obliterated everything from sight except the
highest peaks in the toe of Italy, and familiar
Stromboli, seventy miles away, which appeared like a
purple island in the snowy sea. Huge and glowing
the red disk rose above the white blanket, spangling
it with showers of gold. Then the Sun God, pleased
with us because we had not harmed his cattle at
Taormina, dismissed the clouds as if by magic order
and gradually spread all Sicily before our grateful
eyes,—Scylla and Charybdis, all of Æolus' seven
islands, and the north seacoast beneath which Cefalu,
the city of the Læstrygones, lay hidden. Mignon had
Antonio show her exactly where Taormina was. She
wanted to look back into her window from which she
watched this immaculate peak we stood on turn to
rose and silver in the early sun.

In packing for our descent, we discovered that we
still had four of the six pint bottles of champagne
brought all the way from home. What carelessness!
It would be bad luck to carry them back again. So
I opened all four and gave one to each of our quartet

with the suggestion that we race to see which of us could drink up his bottle first.

Antonio won without trying. I took second honors, while Jimmy and Min were merely "also ran's." This generous and sudden quaff at the thin altitude of nine thousand seven hundred feet had an amazing effect on Madonna-faced Min. She spread her blanket on the observatory floor and did the most surprising Oriental dance upon it. On the way down the mountain she said that by looking intently to the east she could see the swaying minarets of Constantinople quite plainly. I told her I believed it because by looking intently to the west I could see Pike's Peak. Jimmy said that no matter how intently she looked, all she could see was stars.

Back in Nicolosi we found that our motor-car, this time, was intact. Before abandoning it we had removed all the removable parts and locked them in the hotel safe.

On the return to Taormina I faced the inevitable,—some immediate decision in regard to my next move. This long unanticipated delay in Sicily had thrown me weeks behind my schedule. November was half gone, and Ulysses, facing the judgment of Zeus, in his doomed ship was still far from home. If I hoped to complete my Odyssean expedition before Christmas, I must be off, and at once.

But I didn't want to be off. I wanted to stay.

So won away had I been by the enchantments of Taormina I had almost ceased to care what happened to Ulysses. In fact I began secretly to hope that Zeus would include him in the general execution of the guilty cattle-slayers, in order that I might have no reason ever to leave Taormina, and Min, . . . and Jimmy.

For two days I wrestled with temptation. Weaker and weaker grew the call of Ithaca. It was only a barren little island anyway, so "far beyond the wave,"—and Taormina, with its roses, and its companionship, and its sensuous appeal, was near, and real.

By the third day I had surrendered fully to the flesh-pots of the Sun God's city.

That night, lured out into the open by the hypnotic full moon, Jimmy and I sought the Greek Theater, and, climbing to the utmost tier, sat where we could look down upon its columned stage, and out upon land and sea. The shimmering ripples on the Mediterranean strung a phosphorescent ribbon for miles up and down the coast of Sicily. The theater came half back to life in the soft illumination; its scars and devastations faded before the harmony of its perfect lines. With eyes half closed one saw the marble columns all in place once more, and the marble muses filling the empty niches in the walls. To be a picture of overwhelming beauty, it needed but the sound of music from an orchestra, and a ballet of green-draped dryads from the Vale of Tempe dancing on the immaterial stage.

It was a crystal evening, and yet Mount Ætna in the background was robed from base to crater-crest in fold upon fold of billowy, motionless white clouds, that turned the volcano into a vast and gleaming phantom of a mountain, ten times as high, ten times as beautiful, as its earthly self. All the valley at its feet was dark in shadow, but soaring up into the stars like a queenly Himalaya, this cloud-clad specter caught the full radiance of the moon and stood mysteriously out against the sky like a vision from some greater, fairer world.

For a long time Jimmy and I sat without speaking, half hypnotized by the surfeit of loveliness about us. I spoke at last:

"Jimmy—I've decided not to carry on with my expedition. I'm going to stay right here in Taormina—as long as you stay."

"You're going to do no such thing, Dick," she replied emphatically. "Think of the time you've spent, and the progress you've made. And now when your Odyssey is almost complete you'd cast it aside for a few moments of self-indulgence. You've lost your sense of values entirely."

"But Jimmy, to-night I *hate* Ulysses. I hate him because he would take me away from the happiest

days I've ever spent in all my life; and I'm so afraid
that if I go—I'll never see you again."

"Now Dick, you're just getting sentimental. Of
course you'll see me. You'll be passing through
London soon, won't you, on your way home? I'll try
my best to be there because I'd like to show you about
England; and then too— " she hesitated for a
moment as if weighing her words, "it will be a good
chance for you to meet my husband."

"Your—your *what!*" I gasped.

"Oh, my husband. He's a jolly old thing, and
lets me dash about as I please. Probably I should
have mentioned him before, but you and I were hav·
ing such fun under the illusion that I was Miss Jimmy
I just couldn't spoil everything."

"I don't believe it, Jimmy," I said disconsolately.
"You're inventing him to drive me away. You
couldn't have kept such a secret from me all this
time. I'd have learned it somehow."

"It is true, Dick." Jimmy's voice was very calm.
"I told Mignon to help me keep the secret. I would
not have told you even now had you been sensible
about your Odyssey. But Dick, it really doesn't
matter, does it?"

For several moments I was too confused and too
dejected to speak. "No—o," I finally replied faintly.
"It shouldn't matter, I suppose,—since I've been de·
ceiving you all along too."

"What do you mean!" Jimmy exclaimed with some agitation.

"Oh, about my own wife," I lied glibly. "She's on her way to Paris now—and expects me to join her there for Christmas. I thought I might stay here, though, until that time. It would be amusing, wouldn't it, if we could arrange for your husband to meet my wife?"

I do not know whether she believed me or not,— most likely she didn't. Men are so ineffective when they try to lie to women. On the other hand I was quite inclined to believe her,—or rather almost believe, although since then I've begun to suspect the husband may have been only a gesture on her part made solely and bravely for the good purpose of putting an end to the demoralizing sentimentality which was threatening to wreck my glorious adventure. However, my Jimmy, if you ever chance upon this tale of our Italian idyl, let me whisper to you here that if your husband *was* just a diplomatic maneuver, so was my wife only an invention of my pride; and let me confess to you now, husband or no husband, that whenever I see the starlight rippling on the sea, or a mountain in the distance robed in clouds, or whenever I see two true blue eyes laughing impishly at me, there's a tug at my heart for Sicily, and the city of the Sun God, and moonlit Mount Ætna and you.

# FIFI PLAYS CALYPSO

# CHAPTER XIX

## FIFI PLAYS CALYPSO

THE chariot of Jupiter rumbled in the far heavens. Black clouds loomed on the horizon, and a sudden cool wind swelled the sails of Ulysses' flying ship. Though Ætna was hardly out of sight, another storm was at hand. Jupiter had promised Helios to avenge the slaughtered cattle and had passed a sentence of death on every guilty Greek. Thundering down upon the doomed vessel he rent it in pieces; and the thirty-one Ithacans, all that remained of the original hundred who had set sail in this same ship thirteen years before, perished in the waves.

Only Ulysses was spared, for he had taken no part in the destruction of Helios' cattle. Clinging to the floating keel, he was borne away by the currents and carried back up the Sicilian coast straight into the roaring Charybdis. By another one of those rather convenient miracles, Homer preserves his hero from the whirlpool, and sends him south again on the changing tides.

**319**

Past Taormina, past Ætna, past Syracuse and the southern end of Sicily he was carried, still clinging to his raft. For nine days he was tossed by wind and wave. On the tenth the pitying gods stranded him, more dead than alive, upon the beach of Ogygia, the island now called Gozo, close to Malta, where Calypso, the goddess of mortal speech, rescued and revived him.*

And on this island, in the cave-dwelling of Calypso, Ulysses was kept an unwilling prisoner by the amorous goddess who had fallen in love with this handsome, heaven-sent Greek, and who, for seven long hateful years, was deaf to all his pleas that she send him on to his yearned-for Ithaca.

Seven years! What a long time to have to live with a goddess. It is no wonder Ulysses was so disconsolate. Goddesses have absolutely no sense of humor. They never laugh delightfully. In fact I never heard of one laughing at all. They are usually big healthy women who go around wearing bronze helmets and carrying spears,—and that would get on any man's nerves. Of course Venus was a welcome exception to all this. She had curly hair, and a beautiful complexion, and feminine allure. If *she* had been in Calypso's place, Ulysses probably wouldn't have

---

*While there has been serious disagreement among students as to the geographical location of Ogygia, sacred local tradition, backed by the fact that Gozo is in the path of currents flowing south from Charybdis, should give this island first claim to the honor.

grumbled so much. But including even Venus, I think goddesses would be deadly bores after a week or two. I'd prefer Jimmy any day.

And *especially* on the day I left Taormina. The train took me down the Sicilian coast to Syracuse, passing en route along the familiar slopes of Ætna, slopes which reminded me every time I looked up at them of Min and Jimmy, and the jolly chilly hours we spent on top.

I had allowed Ulysses to return to Charybdis with-out my following him. One encounter with that strip of cold swirling water had been so much more than sufficient for me that had I found myself being carried back for a second visit I should have been just as alarmed as he was. I was on my way to Malta with Ulysses' whirlpool episode scrupulously left out.

As I had stuck to "blubber" and champagne at Taormina and left Helios' precious cattle strictly alone, the Sun God had no reason to be wroth with me, nor Jupiter to use my Malta-bound ship as a target for lightning practise. In consequence, the voyage was utterly dull,—so dull in fact, I was sorry I had been so virtuous.

Comfortably lodged in Valetta, the chief port of Malta and one of the great British naval stations, I set out in quest of information concerning Gozo and Calypso's cave. Overtaking an intelligent and cour-teous-looking gentleman, I stopped to ask for directions to the American consulate where such information might be found.

"I'll show you the way," he said pleasantly. "I happen to be going there myself. It's only a block."

"Do you know the consul?" I inquired as we walked along. "I've a lot of foolish questions to ask him; so I hope he'll be in a good humor."

"Oh yes, I know him quite well," he laughed. "You're lucky if he's even civil to you to-day. His disposition is dreadful on Thursdays."

"Is it better on Fridays? I might wait and come back to-morrow."

"Oh, I wouldn't humor him that way. He's spoiled enough already."

"How awful to have grouchy people for consuls," I said. "He'll probably make me wait all morning."

"And there's nothing for you to read in the waiting-room but economic statistics and the *Pipe and Valve Review*," he lamented. "And the chairs are enough to give one spinal meningitis."

As we got to the door I held back.

"Honestly, you've frightened me so I don't dare go in."

"Oh, come along," he urged. "I'll see that the ogre doesn't eat you."

In the reception room a secretary bowed to the floor as we entered.

"What fine secretaries!" I thought to myself.

My companion led me straight into the consul's office, and sat in the consul's chair behind the consul's desk, and offered me one of the consul's cigarettes.

"Now, sir," he said with mock pompousness, "the American consul is at your service."

And then and there we laughed our way into a rast friendship. His disposition on Thursdays was charming. He took me to lunch that very noon in an exquisite club built in the sixteenth century as quarters for one of the orders of the celebrated Knights of Malta. We dined and we tramped; we talked without ceasing; and there was not an inch of road over the curious, colorful, historic little island our motor did not traverse.

Several days after my arrival a friend of the consul gave me a tea party and asked every American in sight. They were a variegated lot: commercial agents, the officers of a passing ship, a family or two residing in Malta for the winter, and a few wandering tourists.

Of this last group was Fifi. Fifi wasn't a day over sixty-five, but that didn't keep us from falling in love at first sight. If her smartly bobbed hair had turned gray, nobody was ever going to know it; and if she couldn't dance the Charleston it wasn't because she didn't try hard enough. Her seven grandchildren were all safely at boarding school; her third husband had been worn out trying to keep up with this in-

defatigible globe-trotter, and left behind somewhere
to recuperate.  She was a freed-woman at last, and
certainly took advantage of it.

After the first cocktail we were so well acquainted
I was smoking her cigarettes and she was fishing for
the olive in my glass.  Two cocktails, and Fifi had
confided in me that she had been a great and good
actress, and could play Ophelia in pink gauze *right
now*.  Three cocktails and I was urging her to do it.

Fifi's presence in Malta took less explaining than
mine.  Her boat on the way from Africa to Italy had
anchored for a day at Valetta, and she was so
intrigued by the picturesque harbor that she had got
off all alone, and stayed.  That was two weeks before.
I told her about my Odyssey and my quest at the
time-being for Calypso's cave.  I was just about to
add that I wasn't overly eager to visit the cave as
I was sure there wouldn't be any Calypso there for
me to play with even if I did find it—when the inspiration came to substitute Fifi for the missing
character.

"Oh, madame," I exclaimed, "if you'd consider
returning to the drama I've a superb rôle for you,—
a *goddess!*  That's much more your type than addle-
pated Ophelias."

"I'd love to," she replied, "only don't call me
'madame,'—that sounds so matronly.  But I'm afraid
I can't accept the part.  I'd planned to leave Malta

to-morrow. I've a fussy old husband in Naples
threatening to divorce me on the grounds of deser-
tion unless I hurry up and join him."

"Aren't you rather accustomed to that by now?"
I said unchivalrously.

"Yes—that's true. I am. And it would be fun
to play a goddess, wouldn't it? As you say, that *is*
my type. Which goddess would I honor?"

"I'll explain. In reliving the *Odyssey* I like to
break it up into acts and scenes according to Homer's
chapters, with myself as the stock hero and usually
most of the cast. Act nineteen is laid in Gozo,—a
little island four miles to the west of Malta. Scene
one is in a cave overlooking the sea. I want you to
be the goddess Calypso who lives there. It's not a
difficult rôle. All you have to do is rescue me from
the waves, fall passionately in love with me, and drag
me unresistingly into your grotto. Of course there
won't be any audience."

"*Well!*—I'm glad of *that!*" said Fifi.

"And there won't be any salary."

"Naturally not! We must keep the drama on a
high moral plane."

"The only description of Calypso Homer gives
us is that she had 'braided tresses,' was 'of mortal
speech,'—and *very* ardent."

"You're right, Dick. I *will* make an ideal
Calypso,—that is, so far as the talking and the ardor

go. I can't very well braid my boyish bob. I'll em‹
phasize the ardor. Then you won't notice my un‹
Homeric coiffure. I'll wire George right away that
I've returned to the stage for a few days, and not to
expect me in Naples till Sunday."

"Good! We'll visit the cave to-morrow morning.
You'll have to go in a dizzy little tug-boat. You
won't mind, Fifi?"

"I won't mind anything if I'm to be a goddess.
Only don't forget the ambrosia—and the nicotine."

Well supplied with both, plus a de luxe basket
luncheon, next day Fifi and I boarded the tug-boat.
The consul wanted to go along as wardrobe mistress
and noises-off-stage, but Fifi wouldn't let him be‹
cause the script didn't call for changes of costume or
departing hoof-beats. I suggested we add a few
nymphs to our cast to attend the goddess. Straightway Calypso had a temperamental outburst, and
insisted such a suggestion plainly showed that already
I had inclinations toward infidelity. In fact she objected so strongly to the nymph idea I didn't dare
even look at the *Queen Elizabeth* when this great
British battle-ship got in our way as we chugged out
of Valetta harbor.

Once we landed at Gozo it was not far to Calypso's
cave. The cabman knew it well, and drove us from
the dock over the flat, treeless little island to the
abrupt headland where the grotto was located.

We came upon the cavern, still called by the name of the goddess, penetrating a great cliff, one hundred feet above the ocean. Measuring some thirty feet square by ten feet high, it was hung with beautifully shaped stalactites, and formed a room where the lady must have found a snug and happy home. Obviously it had been repeatedly used as a dwelling from the most distant age. Signs of the chisel were everywhere. A convenient shelf extended from the door, like a porch, out over the beach. This shelf made an ideal point of observation, so we sat down upon it to rest. Fifi took off her jaunty little toque, and let the wind blow through her close cropped hair; while I tried to picture Ulysses and his raft washing ashore on a curve of sand below, and Calypso, with the cry of "A man! A man!" hurrying down the path to rescue him.

It was a dreamy day. In the open, the December chill was penetrating, but here on the protected sunny ledge one would never have realized that winter— such as it is—was close at hand. The cave and the sea and the solitude brought back memories of a similar (if more turbulent) situation two months before: memories of the Cyclops' land where Leon in the Grotto of Polyphemus related to Rosario, our shepherd-boy host, the tale of Ulysses' encounter with the one-eyed giant. Leon—and his music . . . What had become of him? His letter from Monte Circeo was the last word I had received. Was he

back in Switzerland? Or was he at Milan—with
Rosa? . . . Rosa . . . Such great dark eyes she
had, this simple peasant girl. Had he really taken
her away from the "island"? He might well have—or
he might still be there himself, on the beach, accompanying her sweet singing with his violin. What a
comic little drama that was at San Felice—our
solemn contest between beads and Beethoven, silk
stockings and Tschaikowsky—and the noble triumph
of music over money. Suddenly I laughed aloud.

Fifi looked at me quizzically.

"What *do* you see, Dick, that's so funny?"

"I see an Italian peasant girl scorning my vast
riches and my knightly love for a barelegged Swiss
minstrel."

"And you laugh? Her husband must have put
poison in your rival's spaghetti."

Before I had finished explaining that this wasn't
the case, I had told her the entire story of Rosa. In
fact there wasn't much I didn't tell her during the
hours we loitered before the cave. Fifi had a subtle
yet irresistible way of wheedling out of me all my past
she thought might be worth hearing. Self-possessed
older women can always do that with younger men
they are fond of. Whenever I began to regret my
expansiveness she shattered all resistance by remind-
ing me that that she had a grandson my age, and that
she was just a sympathetic old lady who had been sent
by heaven for me to confide in.

At twenty-six, I hadn't had an *especially* crimson record to confess.  However I wasn't going to disappoint her by admitting it.  Fifi never listened to a more profligate autobiography than the one I made up and related to her on the porch of Calypso's cave.  Of course she was far too sophisticated to believe me entirely.  It gave her a great thrill nevertheless—as it gave me—to hear the heart-wrung revelations of my scarlet years.

She learned that my life had been just one long series of passionate episodes.  And, oh, how I had suffered!  I had flung myself into my present expedition in a desperate effort to overcome the melancholia to which a recently broken heart had driven me.  I'd never heard myself wax so eloquent.

"What a beastly thing love is!" I exclaimed, inspired by her rapt attention.  "How wretchedly, deliberately perverse!  Look at Circe and Calypso and Ulysses.  Circe, who tried to turn him into a pig, he loved completely.  He lived a year in her palace, was the father of her son, and was made to leave her only under pressure.  But Calypso—who saved his life when he was cast by the sea on the beach down there, who brought him up here to the shelter of her cave, nursed him back to life, loved him with all her heart, and promised him eternal youth if he would only forget Penelope and live with her forever—Calypso, he scorned.  Why is it that those we hunger for never love us, and those that do, leave us cold as ice? Why must people live and love in profile? Why must each one turn away his eyes from the one that loves him to some one ahead who instead of looking back squarely, only yearns for the next in line? Profile—profile! Oh, Fifi, is there no full-faced love?"

Fifi was simply palpitating when lack of breath made me conclude my outburst. Never with all her three husbands had she heard such a *cri du cœur.* It was just too marvelous. She insisted on my telling her more about love, but that was all I knew about it, so I tried to side-track the subject.

"Fifi, you're not playing your rôle of the Goddess Calypso ardently enough. You're letting your Ulysses jabber away by the hour without a thought for his comfort. It's two o'clock, and you've not even fed him lunch,—much less ambrosia."

"Well, it's your own fault. How do you expect me to think about bread and beans when you are ensnaring beautiful women? I *have* been neglectful though. Here's the ambrosia"—she said rummaging in the basket—"and here's a cup. Now put this coat under your head, Ulysses, and Calypso will feed thee."

The basket proved to contain a banquet which the original owner of the cave with all her magic could not have improved upon: caramel cake, and apple tarts, and chocolate bars, and ginger cookies, and tangerines, and olives, and *lots* of ambrosia. We never even got to our stuffed eggs and peanut-butter sandwiches.

I proved especially destructive to ginger cookies. Still clinging to an uneaten fistful I leaned back in the warm sunshine against the cavern wall, with a feeling of benign contentment.

"You know, Goddess," I said, "I think Ulysses was a dub to have left Calypso, if she treated him as well as you treat me. This certainly is the life! What do you say we improve on Homer, and instead of sending me off on a raft, and leaving you here all alone and everything, we sail away together and form a traveling theatrical company? You could play all the Homeric heroines to my Ulysses. There's Princess Nausicaa at Scheria where we'd go straight from here, and there's Queen Penelope at Ithaca. You admit you've never been happy since you left the theater. Here's a chance to come back, and combine your art with your travels. Secretly I've always wanted to be an actor myself. I'm never so happy as when I'm speaking a piece. Of course people might misinterpret our purely professional association. But you wouldn't mind if it caused a little scandal in Malta, would you?"

"Mind it!—I'd be *proud* of it at my age, Dickie. Only tell me—before I sign the contract—where is this Scheria place? I can't go to the Arctic, or the Indies,—not if you're traveling on that raft you mentioned. I've got to go to Naples, if I'm ever going to meet my husband."

"That's perfect! Scheria is the island of Corfu, and it's only a few hours from the heel of Italy. It's not much out of your way,—that is, not much if you want to go."

"I do want to go, Dick. I'd love to keep on playing Homer—it's so dignified; and I've always wanted to see Corfu. The island must be beautiful from what I hear. If only it weren't for George—he's been sending me more and more disagreeable cables every day. I was supposed to reach Naples a week ago. He's probably already excommunicated me for the wire I sent him yesterday postponing my sailing once more."

"But, Fifi, you'll never have this chance to act again. George is no doubt as mad already as he can get, so a few more days' delay won't make him any madder. If you'll join my company I'll co-star you. Just think, that might even lead to the movies!"

"I know it. But, Dick, I'm almost broke, and under the circumstances George would *never* send me any money for a trip to any place except Naples— especially if he thought I was running off with an actor."

Driven to it by her stubbornness I played the card I had been holding back in case she refused to respond to reason:

"Fifi, if you'll go on to Corfu with me like a good girl, and play Nausicaa, I'll tell you some things about my love life that are just so *terrible* I couldn't even mention them to-day."

"Oh, I'll go! I'll go!" Fifi exclaimed hurriedly.

# THE PRINCESS

# CHAPTER XX

AND what's more, Fifi *did* go.  George continued to wait in Naples while his gallivanting wife continued her relapse into the drama.  He waited while we embarked at Malta, shortly after our visit to Gozo, on a liner bound for Triest; and he waited while we changed boats at Brindisi in order to cross the Adriatic from Italy to Corfu.

The second boat was a dreadful little tub.  Fifi's stateroom proved so stuffy I sat up with her on deck most of the one night we had to endure the voyage, and in the cold starlight, to keep her from regretting our escapade, further analyzed the intricacies of love.

"You remember, Fifi, what I said at Gozo about people always loving in profile?—and about the Circe-Ulysses-Calypso triangle?  Well, the usual thing happened at Corfu, when Ulysses arrived there and met Princess Nausicaa."

"Who got pursued then?"

"Ulysses, again.  She was mad about him, and

337

so, of course, he was bored with her. 'Nausicaa' is
a fine dramatic rôle. Your interpretation of a goddess showed such talent I'm expecting great things
of you as the young Greek princess."

"Must I always be cast as the disappointed
woman?" Fifi asked.

"But that's the only part in this act worthy of
your genius—unless you want to be an attendant
maiden, or the princess' middle-aged mother. If
you'll go on to Ithaca I'll cast you as Penelope.
Think of my sensational home-coming—with all my
demonstrations of faithfulness to you after twenty
years' absence! That should compensate for the dis-
appointments at Gozo and Corfu."

"All right, I'll play; only I wish you'd tell me
more about this princess part—and the plot. Must I
have braided tresses again, and be of mortal speech?"

"Not any more. This time you are a pure maiden
about eighteen. You must be able to drive a team of
mules well, play ball, and do the family wash."

"Ye gods, Dickie!—While I'm at first base scrub-
bing shirts, what are you doing?"

"Why, I've come on a raft from the cave of
Calypso. Jupiter persuaded her to send me home to
Ithaca. On the way there Neptune raises a storm
and destroys my raft, and I have to swim two days
before the waves fling me up on the west coast of
Corfu. You see I'd blinded his son, Polyphemus,
nine years before. and he had a long memory   ]

crawl ashore covered with beard and brine, and stumble into a thicket of trees to sleep.

"Now here's where *you* enter—driving a mule-wagon piled high with soiled linen, and surrounded by court maidens. You and the other girls launder everything in the little stream that flows into the bay there, and while the clothes are drying, several of you play with a golden ball on the beach. One of the less skilful pitchers throws it into the sea, and everybody screams and shouts.

"In my grove of trees I am awakened by the noise, and walk forth to find out what it's all about. I'm so wild-looking, and so undressed, the maidens fly in terror down the beach—except you."

"But Dick, shouldn't I fly too—to be—er—modest?"

"Of course not. You're a princess, and very brave. Nothing disconcerts you."

"Do you think this act will get by the Board of Censors?"

"Why shouldn't it? Didn't Homer write it? And isn't it a classic?"

"Well, go on. What happens next?"

"Nausicaa sees that Ulysses is a helpless suffering castaway, and takes pity on him. She gives him a tunic—or whatever it is Greeks wore—and has him follow the wagon to her father's palace. There she falls in love with the stranger. No harm comes of it, though. Ulysses reveals himself to the king, tells

Nausicaa he'll be a brother to her, is given a regular bust-up of a banquet, and escorted home in a private yacht. *Now*—how do you like your part?"

"It's improving. Think I'll go back to my state-room with my stockings right away and rehearse the great laundry scene."

Realizing at Corfu City, what objects of gossip theatrical people are at all times, Fifi and I decided to allow the breath of scandal no chance to enter our newly formed company. She found quarters in a delightful hotel with a garden, while I went deco-rously to a pension three blocks away.

For several days we were so occupied with Corfu's poetic setting and colorful people we didn't take Homer too seriously. When, at last, the spirit moved, we secured a 1920 model Ford—shades of an Alice-blue Rolls-Royce—and rode across the island under the endless olive groves to the west shore where Ulysses, coming from Malta, must have landed.

There we found glorious scenery—great five-hundred-foot cliffs stretching out of sight all along the coast, with a single brief interval where the walls relented and made room for a small bay fringed with beach. Being the only beach on the west coast, this had to be Ulysses'.

"Here's the theater, Princess," I said as we climbed out of our motor and reached the sand.

The theater proved rather bare of properties. We couldn't find any stream where Fifi could do the washing,—so we had to leave that out. I had brought along a lemon for the golden ball, but there were no court maidens to throw it at,—so that was left out too. December was well advanced, and the water like ice, so I decided to leave out the part where our hero is cast ashore on a wave. Nor were there any trees for me to come leaping from adorned in beard and brine; and even if I had leaped, my whiskers, carefully un-barbered since last Wednesday, were still not nearly ferocious enough to cause young maidens to go fleeing down the beach, screaming.

In fact the only part of the Homeric parallel we could perform was my acceptance of Nausicaa's invitation to follow her Ford mule-wagon to the palace. Even this wasn't altogether authentic, since in shame-less contradiction to Homer I not only made the princess let me ride on the front seat, but also took over the driving of the team myself when my bene-factress proved inept at keeping the reins clear of the mules' tails.

Whatever liberties we may have taken in eliminat-ing action from the first scene of the act, we more than made up for in the scene at the palace where King Alcinous, Nausicaa's father, gives Ulysses the lavish banquet. True, we didn't have any king, so, to get around this discrepancy, I had the princess give the banquet.

And how well she gave it! Homer would have been more than satisfied with the abandon and the

dramatic genius we put into our acting in the dining-
hall.   Fifi stopped at nothing to make her party
sumptuous and expensive.   She certainly did succeed.
I had indigestion for days afterward.

Toward midnight, when the pheasant from
Albania and the champagne from France had been
exhausted, and we were feeling rather reckless, I
secured a skiff, and rowed Fifi out to the islet in the
harbor known as "Ulysses' Ship."   Tradition de-
clares that Neptune was so vexed with the Scherian
sailors for having escorted Ulysses safely back to
Ithaca, he struck the returning vessel with a thunderbolt as it entered the home-port, and turned it, and
all its mariners, to rock.   The islet is on the opposite
side of Corfu from the Homeric city, but let's not
notice such a little inconsistency;—the story is too
sacred, and the island, beneath its ancient cypresses,
too lovely.

Fifi and I bumped ashore, and, moving cautiously
through the dense dark grove, found the chapel built
on the island's "fo'castle."   Here, beneath the chapel
walls, we rested.   The night, and the stars, and the
wind through the cypresses, and the shadow of the
ghostly little shrine, all made me feel so religious I
obeyed the impulse to confess to Fifi whatever of my
sins she had not extracted before.   I was under obliga-
tion to her anyway for the banquet, and when she
reminded me that she was just a "sympathetic old
lady sent by heaven to comfort my distresses," I

realized that a confessional was a highly acceptable way to pay my debt. With appropriate sighs and tears I recited the last two chapters from my past that had been tenaciously withheld before—the story of the girl in Argentina who shot herself when I skipped the country—and the awful scandal that had caused me to be expelled from Oxford. Of course I'd never been near either place, but that only gave my imagination added freedom for there were no realities to inhibit me. My conscience had not enjoyed such a thorough cleansing in years. It was three o'clock in the morning before the corpse was buried, and I felt sufficiently consoled and absolved by High Priestess Fifi to lead her stumblingly back to the skiff.

As I rowed away toward home, Fifi sank wearily on to the bottom of our boat. All day long I had ignored the fact that with all her sporting spirits, she was not the girl she used to be forty years ago, and I had dragged her about mercilessly since early morning. And yet, even then, as she rested her head on the gunwale, and the wind fluttered through her hair, and the dim starlight softened her features, she did not appear to be half her age.

"Fifi," I said, "I understand now how well you must have played Ophelia. In that position you look just like her."

"Ophelia! My God!" she exclaimed with a groan of utter exhaustion, "—you mean King Lear!"

# ULYSSES RETURNS

# CHAPTER XXI

## ULYSSES RETURNS

On the day Fifi and I had glorified the drama on the Corfu beach, I had climbed to the top of a headland and looked south, down the rocky coast toward Ithaca, only a hundred miles away. And as I looked I caught something of Ulysses' own spirit of impatience. Ithaca! Ithaca! For six months I had been on my way to Ithaca, and now at last it was just beyond the horizon. My pulse beat a bit faster at the thought, for I knew at this point what Ulysses did not know,—that the greatest test of his courage and resourcefulness was to be in his own castle. Standing on the cliff above the bay I could see the harbor where Nausicaa's city had stood, and could picture Ulysses in a swift Scherian ship sailing forth from it, speeding southward through the night, and landing at Ithaca at dawn.

I must go on,—and alone, for the next morning after our visit to "Ulysses' Ship," an ultimatum-ish cablegram came from George (instead of the thou-

sand lire Fifi had wired for) demanding that his per-
egrinating wife abandon the drama and return to
private life.  As unreasonable as his cable was, Fifi
realized his patience was quite exhausted, and that she
had best not tax it further by going on with me beyond Corfu.  It was a sad decision.  Never would
she play Penelope now.  She must say farewell to
Homer and go back to George.

Somewhat annoyed with Ulysses for his willing-
ness to leave behind such agreeable company as
Nausicaa's, I sailed away from Scheria and sped
southward through the night, just as my great example had done.  At dawn I looked from a porthole.
There was my island, mountainous, gray, immortal.
"I live on clear-seen Ithaca, wherein is a mountain,
Neriton," Ulysses had told King Alcinous.  And
there was Neriton, rising majestically above me.

I go ashore in the Bay of Vathy,—the very shore
where Ulysses was landed by the Scherian sailors.
I deposit my baggage at the little hotel.  Burdened
with only a large map of Ithaca and my faithful
pocket *Odyssey,* I strike out down the beach to the
place where Athena, Ulysses' best friend among the
gods, comes to aid him.  She is aware of the fact that
a swarm of insolent suitors of Penelope are living
wantonly in his castle, and that he must approach
cautiously and incognito.

Disguising Ulysses as an aged beggar, Athena

assists him store his Scherian gifts in a cave overlooking the bay, and then tells him to go to the Rock of Korax, to seek his old swineherd, Eumæus, who is still faithful.

I find the cave,—exactly as it is described in the *Odyssey*. From there, on the pages of my book, I see the transformed Ulysses start toward Eumæus' hut.

I am right behind him. By means of a mountain path we reach the Rock of Korax, "a place of wide prospect." From it I can see the coast of Greece, twenty miles to the east, and there, far away, and high, gleams the snowy summit of Parnassus rising above the clouds. Parnassus!—where I had prayed to Apollo, months before, to guide and encourage his humble supplicant in order that I might reach Ithaca in safety. Considering everything I think Apollo did very well by me. In fact I promised him right there on the Rock of Korax, that if he would only see to it that this book, in which he was going to be frequently mentioned, turned out to be a readable and a worthy book, I'd build a temple to him in Central Park.

As the old beggar approaches the hut of Eumæus, several huge dogs rush out upon him. Ulysses wisely sits down on the ground and drops his staff. As I approach the hut of a modern swineherd on the same plateau, several huge dogs rush out at me. Imitating

Ulysses I sit down on the ground and drop my walking stick until the yelping animals are called off.

By the swineherd's hearth Ulysses meets Telemachus, now grown to manhood, and reveals himself to his son. Then he learns that Penelope's suitors are not ten, nor twenty, but over a hundred, all living like leeches upon the absent king's estate, and refusing to disband till Penelope has chosen one to be her husband.

Father and son, vowing that these invaders must pay for their crimes with their lives, depart for the palace. With one eye on my book, and one on the path, I follow Ulysses once more.

It is a nine-mile walk to the Homeric city,—up and over the narrow isthmus which connects the two sections of the island. The site of the royal home is on a flat hilltop overlooking the little Bay of Polis from which the twelve Ithacan ships and twelve hundred men had sailed away to Troy.

At the door of the court Ulysses comes across an aged dog, Argus, whom in the old days he had reared with his own hands. Argus must have been just a pup when Ulysses went away, for twenty years had intervened, but even so the faithful animal had not forgotten the man who had been kind to him.

When the beggar speaks, Argus knows the voice. Twenty years he had waited. And now his master has come home at last. He tries to raise his head and crawl toward him, but he has not the strength. Feebly he wags his tail, and drops his ears, and whines pitifully, and dies at Ulysses' feet.

Then—so reads my *Odyssey*—the beggar enters the great hall. It is filled with a hundred roystering men. There is loud drunken laughter, and smoke from the open fires, and motion and uproar everywhere. The king of Ithaca who had left his home so well ordered, so happy, returns to this wanton scene, and to the wreckage of his household.

In my fancy I slip into the hall and climb into a balcony where I can sit and watch the growing drama. All through the evening the suitors continue their revels, and at midnight reel out to find their quarters.

Meanwhile, Penelope, in her apartment, has given way to despair. Ulysses would never come. To-morrow she would agree to marry any one of the suitors who, with Ulysses' bow, best shot an arrow at the mark.

And next day she sets about to make good her resolution. As my pages turn I see her enter the hall with the bow and quiver. I see the bow go the rounds—unbent, until the beggar asks for a trial. There is a storm of indignation. Penelope insists the old man's request be granted. I hold my breath. I know what is coming. Penelope leaves the hall at Telemachus' insistence. My eyes are racing down the page.

Ulysses puts an arrow on the string, and sends it flying at the mark. The suitors, with a cry of astonishment, leap to their feet . . . and in my balcony I see myself leap to mine. I see Ulysses, standing at the end of the hall, tearing off his rags. Like an enraged lion he glares at his enemies. I see Antinous, the arrogant leader of the band, with a bowl of wine raised to his lips. Ulysses seizes a second arrow. Away goes the shaft—at the human mark. It drives straight through his neck. The blood gushes from his nostrils; the silver cup dashes to the floor; and Antinous plunges on top of it. There is a roar from the suitors . . . with a pounding heart I clutch my little book, and read furiously. . . .

"Dogs!" shouts Ulysses. "Did ye think I should not come back from Troy!"

In consternation the suitors look to the walls for the weapons that have always hung there. Telemachus has removed them all. They run to the doors. Every exit has been tied fast from the outside. Blocked and defenseless they rush at Ulysses with knives. Telemachus strikes them down. The arrows are flying, flying, and slaughtering. The bare dirt floor is red with blood. There are cries of rage and agony. Grim and desperate, father and son face the multitude. A shower of missiles is flung at Ulysses. Athena turns them all away. Then the suitors know that they are doomed, for the gods are fighting on the other side. Like maddened cattle they try to escape. There is no escape. Splashed crimson, Ulysses piles the dead on the dying. The banquet hall becomes a shambles of butchery and death. I see myself grow sick and faint from the holocaust below. Nothing stays Ulysses' vengeance, not while one cursed suitor lives. Gasping, gory, crazed with blood-lust, he stands in the middle of the carnage.

Still clinging, in my fancy, to my balcony, I see Ulysses' servants rehabilitating the slaughter-house. The bodies are dragged out; the benches purified. Cleansed of his bloody rags, but still disguised, Ulysses awaits Penelope. Some one has gone to tell her that the King of Ithaca has returned.

Incredulous, hesitating, Penelope comes into the hall. Can this beggar be her husband? Is it not one more groundless rumor? And then Athena, in this last need of her favorite, lays her hand upon his head, and before my very eyes, the disguise falls away. The Ulysses that I have been pursuing these many weeks, the Ulysses that Penelope has been waiting for these twenty years, young, strong, heroic, stands before us. In tears Penelope melts into her husband's arms, and he holds her there, tenderly.

The last scene of Homer's epic poem has been played, the last page read. I close the book regretfully, and turn my eyes from the precious little volume to the sunset which, viewed through the shining olive trees on Ulysses' castle site, is enflaming the western sea.    Never had I known a sky to be so radiant, so gold,—a glorious end of a glorious day and of an immortal story.    On such a scarlet sky as this, three thousand years ago, Ulysses and Penelope, reunited, had watched the darkness creep.

And now, once more, the darkness creeps on Ithaca—and me.    The scarlet fades.    The evening stars come out.    Peacefully falls the curtain of my play.    I pocket my faithful little book and leave the twilit stage.    My Odyssey—is ended.

**THE END**

Some of the other titles in the Adventure Travel Classic series published by The Long Riders' Guild Press. We are constantly adding to our collection, so for an up-to-date list please visit our website: **www.thelongridersguild.com**

| | |
|---|---|
| The Rob Roy on the Jordan | John MacGregor |
| In the Forbidden Land | Henry Savage Landor |
| From Paris to New York by Land | Harry de Windt |
| My Life as an Explorer | Sven Hedin |
| Elephant Bill | Lt.-Col. J. H. Williams |
| Fifty Years below Zero | Charles Brower |
| Quest for the Lost City | Dana and Ginger Lamb |
| Enchanted Vagabonds | Dana Lamb |
| Seven League Boots | Richard Halliburton |
| The Flying Carpet | Richard Halliburton |
| New Worlds to Conquer | Richard Halliburton |
| The Glorious Adventure | Richard Halliburton |
| The Royal Road to Romance | Richard Halliburton |
| My Khyber Marriage | Morag Murray Abdullah |
| Khyber Caravan | Gordon Sinclair |
| Servant of Sahibs | Rassul Galwan |
| Beyond Khyber Pass | Lowell Thomas |
| True Stories of Modern Explorers | B. Webster Smith |
| Call to Adventure | Robert Spiers Benjamin |
| Heroes of Modern Adventure | T. C. Bridges |
| Death by Moonlight | Robert Henriques |
| To Lhasa in Disguise | William McGovern |
| The Lives of a Bengal Lancer | Francis Yeats-Brown |
| Twenty Thousand Miles in a Flying Boat | Sir Alan Cobham |
| The Secret of the Sahara: Kufara | Rosita Forbes |
| Forbidden Road: Kabul to Samarkand | Rosita Forbes |
| I Married Adventure | Osa Johnson |
| Grey Maiden | Arthur Howden Smith |
| Sufferings in Africa | Captain James Riley |
| Tex O'Reilly – Born to Raise Hell | Tex O'Reilly and Lowell Thomas |

The Long Riders' Guild
The world's leading source of information regarding equestrian exploration!
**www.thelongridersguild.com**

Printed in the United States
38741LVS00004B

9 781590 480847